THE BIG BOOK OF
PASTA

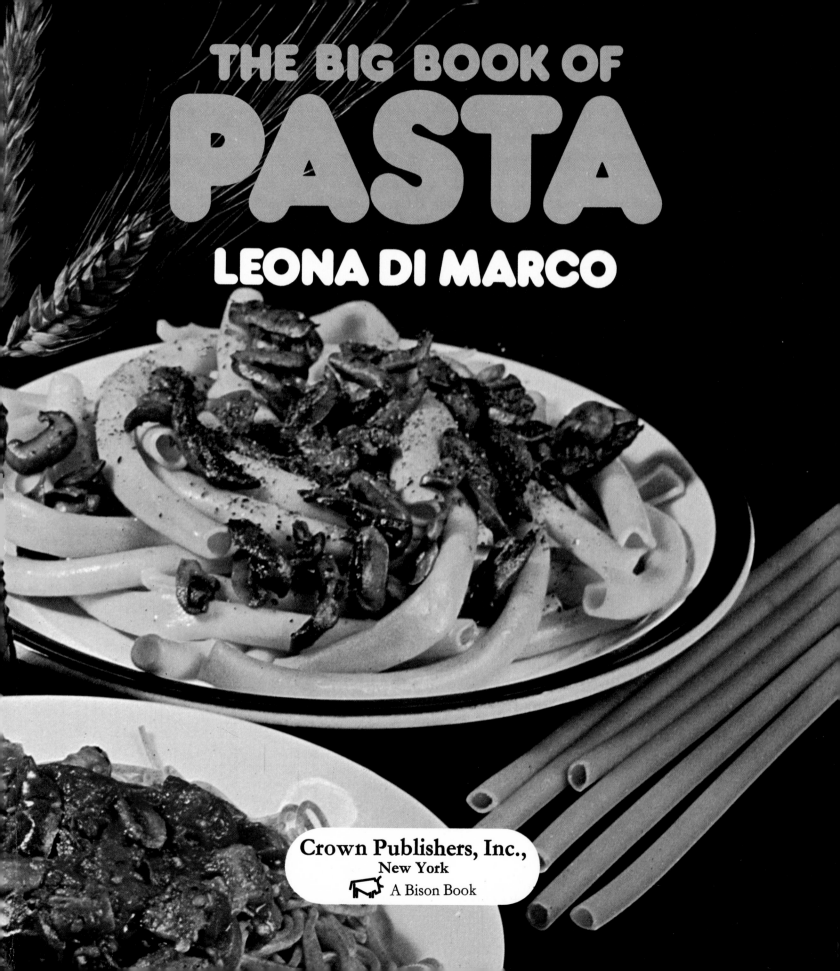

THE BIG BOOK OF
PASTA

LEONA DI MARCO

Crown Publishers, Inc.,
New York

A Bison Book

First published in the USA in 1977 by
Crown Publishers, Inc.
© Copyright Bison Books Limited, London, England

ISBN: 0-517-52916-5

No part of this publication may be reproduced
without the permission of the publishers.

Printed in Hong Kong

Library of Congress Cataloging in Publication Data
Di Marco, Leona
The Big Book of Pasta
A Bison Book
1. Cookery (Macaroni) I. Title
TX809.M17D56   641.8'22   77-2184

Previous page
A Pasta Trio
Spaghetti with Pine Nuts(*left*)
Zitoni and Mushrooms(*right*)
Wholemeal Spaghetti with Eggplant and Pepper Sauce (*center*)

For my Mother and Father
– in thanks for a good beginning

CONTENTS

Acknowledgments

I would like to thank the following women for their helpful quest for old family recipes: Mary Brindisi, Harriet Marks, Vera Doll, Ruth Marks, Marie Panella Jones and Ruby Conarro.

I would like to thank Julie Koppel and Elma White for their photography of the food of Ballena Blanca—they were most helpful. Win Wells did all the line drawings which supplement the text. I am also eternally grateful to Derick Whitty who is responsible for all the other photographs.

I appreciated the technical and wise comments of Mary Summers, Kathlyn Tierney, Win Wells and Maggie Kopola in the final stages of the book.

Thursday Night is Spaghetti Night

Until I left home for university, I never realized there could possibly be an indifferent cook, or even more incredible, an unappetizing meal! I was surrounded from birth by warm, loving women who were, I now realize, inspired and creative cooks.

Although my mother was of what we euphemistically called in the twenties an 'American' background, she quite sensibly upon taking her marriage vows, immediately embraced the delights of Italian cooking. Initially, she was taught by my father's sister, my beloved Aunt Theresa Amarosa, who although now deceased, I'm sure is cooking pots of spaghetti for all the angels that must surround her in heaven. Mother's education was furthered by her newly made friends in the Italian community of Utica, New York. The novice soon became the doyenne.

The rich ambiance of an Italian-American home was mine. Memories of my childhood are highlighted by scents, sounds and succulent foods, originating in that most wonderful of rooms, the kitchen. The enriched aromas floated upwards to my private world, pulled me away from the latest Bobbsey Twins adventure, impelled me to leave my fantasies and daydreams and descend the stairs to the warmth of the kitchen. This room was the hub of my life as a child. Wonderful women, friends, button-hole aunts, gathered together to share their recipes—combining their talents into a gastronomic whole. Their greatest joy was to prepare and cook delicious meals for their families.

I sat entranced, arms on the table and watched the preparation of the food: sauces gently cooking, strong arms rolling out thin sheets of pasta, ribbons of spaghetti emerging from the ancient black iron macaroni machine. Large rounds of egg-yellow pasta resting under bowls, was soon cut and shaped into small sausage rolls that emerged between the rollers of the machine in long strands. The pasta was gently caught by loving fingers and carefully carried to the bedroom. It was laid out, strand by strand, on the white sheet covering the bed. A few minutes later the ladies ceremoniously paraded back to the bedroom, gathered the dried spaghetti and then dropped them, one by one, into the large kettle, bubbling furiously with salted boiling water.

The large, heavy iron Dutch Oven was filled with the pungently scented cooking sauce. Tiny bubbles emerged, spread and then blended into a rich, thick gravy. Home preserved tomatoes, sweet basil, garlic and olive oil joined together to become what my mother called a 'quick' sauce.

Women's voices, chattering and gossiping, laughed as they patted, arranged and cut the endless ribbons of dough. Pasta, the basis of so many succulent dishes; tiny ravioli filled with fresh ricotta cheese; lasagne layered with a thick meat sauce and a variety of cheeses that had been arranged in small dishes, like a drugstore sandwich counter, for easy assembly.

11

Let me talk of the cheeses we used: the thin slices of mozzarella that were cut from the little pot-bellied shapes, still wet from their damp paper home. I still am amazed that the square slabs of plastic-covered mozzarella, in the supermarkets today taste like the wet, salted original, when cooked. Ricotta was delivered fresh from the dairy next door, still oozing tiny drops of milk through the large tubular shaped colander. The ricotta was gently crushed with a fork, mixed with ground black pepper and garden fresh sprigs of parsley. A mound of freshly grated parmesan cheese appeared under the grater, filling the plate.

But back to pasta. Blobs of potato dough, pressed with a firm thumb and rolled on a hard surface became gnocchi. Fresh tagliatelle, still wet from the boiling water was immediately tossed with butter and grated parmesan cheese. The shapes of pasta and the combination with sauces was endless.

Summers were elongated rays of sunshine. Bushels of tomatoes, soon to be combined with freshly picked sweet basil, were peeled and bottled in the summer cellar kitchen. Freshly seasoned ground pork, stuffed into casings, was preserved in olive oil for future use in sauces. Bushels and pecks of peaches, plums and pears sat stolidly waiting to be preserved into winter desserts.

I grew up with a total love of the kitchen. One of my greatest pleasures today is to cook for and serve extended meals to my family and friends. The preparation and organization used in presenting a memorable feast uses all the administrative skills I have accumulated in the variety of positions I have held in universities and the theater. It is like preparing for a production of a play or organizing the research for a lecture: attention to detail, development and an ample use of creative imagination.

Being Italian-American has been a sustaining joy in my life! I remember a dear old lady who taught sociology in the most delicate manner. The course was entitled Ethnic Minorities. Her butterfly voice trembled with excitement as she declared to the class: 'Can you imagine how it must feel to have two opposite cultures at battle in your chest! Imagine the mixture of an English descendant and perhaps (a long pause) an Italian immigrant!' My friends dutifully turned to me and gazed in awe at my embattled torso. Other Italian-Americans are as obsessed as I am with food. My husband and I were grounded at Newark Airport during a snowstorm and we had to rent a car to drive us to Kennedy Airport to connect with our flight to our home in Spain. The driver was an Italian-American from New Brunswick. The Christmas holidays had just passed and the conversation immediately turned to food as we traveled across Staten Island to Long Island in the snowstorm. We compared our holiday feasts and traditional foods with the consuming passion of all Italian-Americans. We laughed at our mutual need to eat spaghetti on Thursday evenings. We recalled in earlier days that it was Tuesday, Thursday and Sunday. Of course on Sunday, macaroni was followed by a chicken or meat course.

Professional circumstances often find me away from home on Thursday evenings. I long ago solved the problem of my 'womb' food with a survival kit of cold spaghetti, lasagne, cannelloni or whatever I have prepared for my family to eat in my absence. Macaroni and sauce is as good cold as it is warm.

My husband tells me I manifest love through food; perhaps I do. Spaghetti and meatballs have been staple fare at all the cast and production parties I have organized through the years. I know when I have a particularly receptive class at the university I invite them to my home for a lasagne dinner. We usually have a lively time in my classes but I hope my students' earnestness in scholarship is not equated with their desire to fill their stomachs with homemade lasagne.

The purpose of this book is to share with you my love affair with pasta and to stimulate your interest in the history, making and eating of the many recipes I have collected, assimilated and conceived in my thirty years of cooking. I hope from reading this book that Thursday night will become Spaghetti Night for you!

The Origins of Pasta

Whenever I think of the conflict between the Chinese and the Italians claiming the creation of pasta, I visualize a scene in which an elegant Mandarin and an Italian dressed as an organ-grinder, are each holding an end of a long strand of spaghetti, tugging for all their worth. The controversy goes back centuries. I like to think that it reveals the passion to which consumers of pasta can rise in defense of this noble food. Tradition has it that Marco Polo brought the art of noodle making back with him from his travels to China. I have come to the conclusion after researching the beginnings of pasta thoroughly, that the Marco Polo theory is a romantic concept.

There certainly is adequate proof that pasta in some form, was being consumed before the latter part of the 13th century. Pasta had become so popular by the time of Frederick II, the Holy Roman Emperor who chose to reside in Sicily, that he gave it the name macaroni based on the word 'Marcus'—the divine dish. Italians have always liked their food. The cuisine of Italy was shaped by many outside influences but the general diet was formed by the Middle Ages. The Crusaders provided the initial stimulus in the adventure of new tastes when they brought back, for instance, wheat—the basis of pasta—from the Saracens. The spice trade, not the noodle trade, was greatly aided by Marco Polo's venture to China. The Italian Peninsula was also influenced by the various invaders who ran across the boot with great zeal. The corruption of the last Roman Emperors made it quite simple for the barbarians of the North to conquer and govern the many provinces of Italy. The Arabs in their thrust across the Mediterranean touched briefly in Southern Italy and influenced the cuisine— especially sugar-based sweets. When the vegetables and fruits were brought from the New World to Italy they immediately became part of the Italian way of life. Fresh vegetables are adored by Italians in their dishes. Although the tomato is not native to Italy they developed the red fruit we know today from the yellow skinned original, 'the golden apple', brought back by Cortez from Mexico. We have tomato sauce and what would the gnocchi be without the potato? Contemporary Italian cuisine with its wonderful regionalism, is very much a highly refined composite of many outside influences. It became the basis of European cuisine. Even the French, quite softly I'm sure, acknowledge their debt to Italy. Catherine de Medici married the future French king, Henry II in 1533 and brought her own cooks with her to the Court from Florence. The French were not the highly honed gourmets of today and they readily accepted the culinary skills presented to them.

In my opinion what passes for 'the Art of French Cooking' today, outside the various citadels of culinary perfection in France, is an over-use and abuse of sauces and cream to cover a multitude of overcooked sins. It is highly overrated. I have lived and traveled abroad for many years. It seems to me from my observations that the majority of hotel restaurants and many-starred eating establishments around the world conspire, thinking that by printing the menu in French regardless of the local language, to confound the average diner, overwhelmed by the mystique and what he thinks is his own ignorance so that he succumbs, terrified before the Maître d's ill-mannered, well-trained condescension. Vice presidents of multi-national companies, retired company directors—all intelligent, sophisticated, cultivated people—quail before the rudeness of an imported French headwaiter.

I find, and many seasoned travelers agree with me, that the oriental and northern Italian cuisine is the most exquisitely delicate in the world. I'm sure I'm going to have every budding Cordon Bleu cook and followers of Julia Childs' brilliant and erudite teachings, burst into a full howl—a primal scream! All I can say is, eat before you speak and make a rational conclusion. I like all food *al dente:* fresh and when the teeth sink into a morsel they do not sag their way through a confusion of tastes. Vegetables, for instance, should be steamed and the flavor not smothered with a mixture of too many herbs and seasonings. The Japanese, in particular, present their food with a restrained flair that is the essence of eye appeal and taste. Enough of my hobby horse and back to the story of pasta.

Certainly there is adequate reference made to the eating of pasta in literature and historical records in Italy. For instance, in *The Decameron*, it refers to the delight of throwing ravioli down a mountain of parmesan cheese! The Chinese have recipes recorded for noodles and stuffed pasta in their literature and early cookbooks. Like so many other new concepts or inventions, pasta probably evolved at about the same time. It was 'in the air'. The concept of pasta is not difficult. After all, pasta is a mixture of flour and water . . . basically.

My husband purchased my beautiful, stainless steel macaroni machine that had been manufactured in Milano, from a shop in Soho, London. The shopkeeper who served him said: 'You are the first white man to buy this machine'. Obviously my good spouse exclaimed his amazement. The shopkeeper continued: 'Yes, usually we sell them only to Chinese restaurants!' This conversation represents to me the final and ultimate compromise: a Chinese cook using an Italian-made macaroni machine.

That most imaginative of Presidents, Thomas Jefferson, after a trip to Italy, tried to popularize pasta in the United States. However, pasta and his imported wine grape vines did not become part of the American cuisine until much later. Americans did not truly become afficianados of pasta until the first part of the twentieth century when the Italian immigration began in earnest. The majority of the new immigrants were from the southern half of Italy where pasta was the dominant food.

For a good many years it was eaten only in the homes and the small family restaurants that dotted the 'Little Italy' neighborhoods of cities. Gradually, as the gentry 'slummed' in the ghettos of the cities the plate of spaghetti and meatballs became the symbol of the new Italian-American citizen. Gradually, Italian traditional food spread its wings. Spaghetti is now considered one of the most popular dishes that emerged from the large variety of immigrant groups who converged on America, bringing the world's larder to the American table.

Not only in America do you find a large variety of Italian restaurants in the commercial section of a city but all over the world. From the sophisticated capitals of Tokyo, Paris and London to a smaller city like Goteborg, Sweden, you will find the Italian restaurant alongside the other two most popular international cuisines—the Chinese and French restaurants.

I have noted in some cookbooks a recipe for 'American Spaghetti' made with canned tomato soup! Horrors! I hope in this book to stretch your concept from the traditional tomato covered spaghetti to the wealth of pasta recipes incorporating meat, fish and vegetables. Spaghetti and meatballs has, does and will appear regularly as a standard menu in the American home. In the early years it was considered a cheap but nutritious food but hardly accepted as an example of gourmet cooking. I remember when we were doing our Greenwich Village 'bit' in the early sixties that we sought out a small Italian restaurant where Eugene O'Neil purportedly ate when he was living on limited resources years previously. Since we qualified as up and coming, which really means down and out, we were delighted to find that the small ten-tabled restaurant still existed. It cost, I still remember in these days of inflation, fifty cents for a large soup dish of spaghetti with majestic meatballs and sauce. It was delicious—we were delighted.

One Sunday afternoon we were strolling through Washington Square area pushing our lovely daughter in her pram, when we passed the restaurant. We put our noses to the window and looked in. Through the darkened dining area we could see the outlines of the pots and pans on the marble topped counter that separated the kitchen from the main room. A slight movement caught our eye. There, nibbling away with gastronomic gusto was a well-endowed rat having his Sunday lunch. Needless to say we never returned to the restaurant. So much for economy.

The prejudice of the original settlers in America die hard. My beloved mother-in-law, now deceased, descended from an old New York City family. Her habit was to visit us each June for the 'English' season. In between trips to Ascot and luncheons at Claridges she joined my husband one day, for a quick meal at a local Italian restaurant that we frequented. She sat down and looked at the waiter with all the charm that had conquered so many hearts and said: 'I want what all the poor little boys in New York eat'. My husband was mortified. The Italian waiter was baffled. She turned to her son for guidance in this culinary quest and he, most embarrassed, mumbled: 'My mother wants spaghetti'. The waiter fortunately had a sense of humor and roared with laughter. Prejudices die hard.

Pasta has become very popular in many countries. At present, we have our home in the foothills of the Spanish Pyrenees, where we now spend the majority of the year. Two traditional dishes appear on every menu in Catalonia: *Macaroni Italien* and *Cannelloni*. The Macaroni Italien consists of short cut macaroni mixed with a meat sauce. Cannelloni, however, is considered Spain's own invention. Each hamlet in the Barcelona-Tarragona area specializes in different sauces and fillings. These I will tell you about later. Tarragona was a major Roman port in the time of Augustus Caesar and the Italian influence can still be detected in certain dishes and habits.

International supermarkets, large and small, have sections devoted solely to pasta. In Italy, where one rather expects it, there are over one hundred different types of pasta. In Spain, I have counted thirty varieties. Dried tortellini and ravioli can be found everywhere. The tomato, fresh, canned, puréed and in sauces is the most commonly used vegetable in Catalonia. You can purchase cannelloni mix, canned cannelloni and ravioli and little dishes of frozen, cooked cannelloni, covered with a béchamel sauce, ready to be popped into the oven. Soho, in London, dominates the pasta scene but the majority of English supermarkets carry not only domestic but imported Italian pasta.

The American selection of commercially made pasta depends on the section of the country in which you live. Italian neighborhoods usually have a large selection of excellent pasta. For instance, my sister tells me that Palettas' market in San Antonio, Texas, carries a wide variety of imported pasta. Supermarkets usually carry at least the standard and more familiar shapes. However, my parents have retired to the heart of the hill country in Central Texas and the selection of pasta is limited to a single brand of poor quality. It is an 'Americanized' version of a flour blend called pasta. The best commercial pasta should be based on flour made solely from durum wheat. Any package that has on its label *pasta di semolina di grano duro* is a genuine semolina pasta made from durum wheat. If you do have access to imported Italian pasta, try to purchase pasta from the Naples region. Some of the commercial derivations cook up into a glutinous collection of strings that descend and lay in the bottom of the stomach like the battleship *Maine*. If you are unfortunate enough to live in an area with a paucity of pasta, then my dears, roll your own!

Pasta as a Health Food

Pasta is most often thought of as an Italian food. Many countries, however, include pasta as a food staple in their diets. The cuisine of Japan, China and other Far Eastern countries use noodles in some form or other, daily. German style noodles, German Spätzle, Hungarian Veal Paprika and Noodles, Noodles Romanoff, Stroganoff Noodles with Cream are European dishes that have traveled abroad and appear regularly on our menus.

The Italians exploited the culinary potential of pasta with the greatest imagination and have created a food that is now becoming recognized as a health food. I am sure this was not their original intention but the result is a deliciously nutritious food. The glutinous durum wheat, ground into a coarse meal and the bran removed, is rich in nourishment. Good quality pasta contains at least fifteen percent protein and is well endowed with other nutrients. Cooked in combination with vegetable oils, lean meat, cheese or vegetables, pasta is an excellent diet food abounding in a dietitian's delight of minerals, vitamins and other nutritive goodies. This is being confirmed continuously by medical research.

By this time, all Americans must be aware of the high fat content in their diets. The press, magazines and the reports on television constantly reveal to us the hazards involved in continuing to eat our bacon and eggs for breakfast. High fat content in diets is a probable cause of heart disease and cancer. England, however, is just becoming aware of the relationship between diet and disease. Only recently, a leading English Sunday newspaper featured an article on food intake and cancer. The author of the article notes with interest that the population in the southern half of Italy, where pasta is eaten daily, has a much lower incidence of heart disease and cancer. Within Italy itself, the incidence of heart disease is higher in the north where they eat more meat and richer sauces. It is the southern Italian who likes his spaghetti with just a bit of olive oil, anchovies, garlic and perhaps cheese. It is low in fat. One of the foods suggested by the author as part of a low fat content diet but nutritious in food value is spaghetti covered with a simple marinara sauce (p. 138) and sprinkled with cheese. Minutes to make and it is high in nutritive elements.

The Chinese and Japanese also consume pasta in the form of noodles as part of their daily diet. Strips of vegetables, raw fish, meat and fowl are mixed with a pungent broth enriched with soy sauce. Like the southern Italian, they also have a low incidence of heart disease and cancer. The danger of high fat content in your diet becomes more obvious when the Oriental diet becomes westernized. Heart disease and cancer have increased when the diet includes creams, butter and fatty meats. The incidence of disease among the many Far Eastern brides of our servicemen has increased when the women have adopted the high fat content of the American diet. Our diet can be related to the size of our pocket books. The higher the standard of living the higher our intake of the more expensive meats, eggs, cream and richer foods. I was discussing the relationship of diet to heart disease and cancer with our good friend Dr. Miguel Dalmau, Head of Internal Medicine, University of Barcelona Medical School (over a plate of humble lasagne of course) and he concurred: 'Cancer and heart disease are rich men's infirmities'.

Pasta, embellished with fresh vegetables and other nutritious food is a delicious prophylactic against heart disease and cancer.

Pasta and the Calorie Myth

Traveling through the beautiful cities of Italy the appearance of the slim, fashionable Italian female shatters one's prejudice about pasta as a fattening food. These elegant women all consume pasta at least once a day and stay slim. The saying 'you are what you eat' is quite true. I think the more accurate phrasing would be 'you are what you over-eat!'

The day I popped out of my mother's womb the battle of the bulge was on. I was a fatty until I was 20. Finally, finding that all the crash diets, fad diets and envying my eternally eating but slim friends brought no significant loss of weight, I consulted a specialist in obesity. You see, I do not mince words! It has taken me years to use that overpowering word—'obesity'. The cooking in our home was well-balanced, nutritious, and delicious. However, vegetables were usually served with heaps of butter and cream. The cookie jar was always full. I learned then about eating the right foods low in fat content but high in nutritional value. I am sure all of you who have dieted in consultation with a doctor have found that you can eat more food on the approved diet then you could before going on the diet.

One of the most popular weight reducing schemes that now consumes the dietary passions of most of the world includes spaghetti on its list of permitted foods. Eating the wrong food and greed cause overweight. Everyone uses food as energy in varying quantities. Find your calorie norm and do not deviate. Rumor has it that Sophia Loren, the gloriously beautiful film star, carries spaghetti with her wherever she goes on location—her passion for pasta is so great. If true, the daily consumption of pasta has not interfered with her figure.

Most sauces that accompany pasta use very little olive oil or vegetable oil as their base. Flour, cream and butter are not used. Vegetables such as tomatoes, zucchini, peppers, onions, artichokes, cauliflower and cabbage are all low in calories. Cooked lightly with a sensitive touch of herbs these vegetables form a nutritious fat-free sauce for pasta. Pasta, served with a sauce and salad is a perfect food. Pasta is filling—a 2 oz. serving of raw pasta (it doubles in size when cooked) covered with a simple sauce will maintain your energy level far longer with fewer calories, than many of the familiar convenience dishes high in fat content such as grilled cheese sandwiches or our beloved hamburgers and french fries.

Use your common sense: people who need to watch their weight should not follow spaghetti with a meat course. Leave that to your energy-consuming friends. The majority of people take in more food than they can possibly use, resulting in unwanted fat. I remember when I was recovering from a recent operation in a Spanish clinic my delight in learning I would have the normal menu for the day. Consommé and custard daily can be boring! Lunch arrived and I was mesmerized by the tray: broth, spaghetti with a tomato sauce, salad, two grilled lamb chops, carrots, green beans and two huge fresh peaches greeted my amazed stare. My morning stroll up and down the corridor had not given me an appetite equivalent to climbing Everest so I ate only the spaghetti and salad. I asked Dr. Santiago Dexues when he appeared on his daily rounds how the dietitian thought anyone could possibly eat that much food in or out of hospital. He replied that since the Civil War all Spaniards approach the table with a compulsion to eat and are only happy when gorged. I have noticed recently in the Spanish daily papers, full page advertisements for obesity clinics.

The Director General of the British Nutrition Foundation said in the *Evening Standard* of 4th November, 1976 we should eat less fat and replace it with starchy cereal foods, making sure they have a high nutrient content. 'There is a common misconception that anything containing starch is fattening but, weight for weight, starch provides the same amount of calories and protein.'

All food eaten in excess is fattening. You are what you eat so do not blame what you eat for your overweight problem. Eat spaghetti and stay slim.

Cooking Comments

I do not believe in second best. If I do not have the proper ingredients available to me, I do not substitute the original ingredient for something that is 'close to it' and hope the recipe will be a success. It is far better to cook another dish or create a recipe that uses what you do have. In all the recipes in this book use fresh ingredients as much as possible. Take advantage of the seasonal changes in vegetables and you will not have a food-bored family say: 'It's Monday so it's meat loaf and carrots' as they congregate for the evening meal. I prefer fresh herbs and seasonings. Dried herbs are used only if you do not have access to fresh herbs. There is no substitute for instance, for mashed garlic cloves in cooking. You not only have the flavor to lose but the oil, also. Many herbs, grown in your garden or window box can be frozen and used throughout the winter months. Use the best quality olive oil, meats and vegetables. The majority of the recipes in this book are basically economical so do not be thrifty to the point of loosing the taste value of the food. Dry wine, red or white, is the best wine to use for cooking. Buy a good wine; beware of wines sold as cooking wines—they usually are poor vintages blended with a small amount of a basically good wine. If it is not good enough for your palate why impose it on your cooking?

The measurements I give in the recipes are approximate. Eggs differ in size, flour in quality, oils in consistency. I am always befuddled when a recipe calls for a 'medium sized' onion. What is medium? One could have an evening's philosophical discussion about 'what is medium'. The surest way is to taste as you proceed and then to adjust any ingredient. I like piquant food; I do not mean so highly flavored with hot red pepper that it makes the consumer's eyes look like an advance case of a thyroid-related illness. Pasta dishes are enhanced by freshly ground black pepper and nutmeg. If my food has a distinctive flavor that separates it from the same dish cooked elsewhere I would say it is the additional use of a few grains of crushed red pepper in my soups and sauces. Sometimes, regardless of the ingredients, a soup is lacking the perfect taste. A dash of soy sauce, Worcestershire sauce or Tabasco sauce often completes the flavor blend.

Read the recipe through before you begin. Arrange your cooking utensils for easy access. Cut, chop or mince any ingredients that need preparation before you start. Use your common sense. I sometimes believe the best cooks are adventuresome souls who cannot resist putting in that little bit of extra seasoning. I have had literally to measure the ounces and grams contained in a handful to give accurate measures of what had been eye judgments of quantities, a little of this and a little of that to ensure that the recipes in this book—some evolved over years—will be successful for you. The majority of cooks who consistently present delicious flavorsome food, if asked for the recipe of a particular culinary masterpiece usually reply with 'a little oil, a pinch of this' syndrome. Take heart. Develop your own style. Do not treat the kitchen as a laboratory with perfect weights and measures. Enjoy the sensuality of cooking!

Cooking Utensils

Your cooking utensils should be varied, sturdy, of excellent quality, durable and to my mind, colorful. When you purchase new kitchenware, buy the best quality available and it will last for many years. I am still using a set of saucepans and skillets made of a cast iron and aluminium alloy that were given to me thirty-five years ago. I prefer a heavy pan for slow cooking foods. The copper-based pans are more suitable to quick cooking techniques. Replace utensils with equal care. Today there are many oven-proof casseroles and pans that are sturdy, colorful and can be used to serve the food directly from the oven to the table. Some of the new, serrated-edged knives are excellent for slicing and retain their sharpness. The kitchenware department of any store is fun to poke about in. Foreign utensils are much more available to us today and I do think the kitchen cupboard should reflect this internationalism, the more we venture into the cuisines of other countries.

Below I have listed the utensils you will need for preparing the recipes in this book. Remember, the best kitchen utensils you own are your hands.

1 large kettle for boiling pasta—6 to 8 quarts (9 liters)
1 soup kettle—4 to 6 quarts (7 liters)
1 large heavy frying pan with cover
1 medium-sized frying pan with cover
a variety of covered casseroles—1½ to 4 quarts (1.5 to 4 liters)
1 large heavy saucepan with lid (I still use a Dutch oven)
1 colander, large size
1 slotted spoon with a long handle
1 small-holed straining spoon
1 spatula
1 wire whisk
1 double boiler
electric blender (I am still not an absolute convert)
1 3-pronged spaghetti fork with a long handle
1 kitchen fork
1 set of kitchen knives
1 pair of kitchen scissors
4 wooden spoons
1 wooden spatula
1 pastry cutter
1 flour sifter
1 meat tenderizer or mallet
1 set of mixing bowls
measuring spoons
several glass measuring cups
wooden chopping board
pastry board (30 in. by 40 in.) or (75 cm by 100 cm)
2 soup ladles
1 24 in. (600 cm) rolling pin
1 pepper grinder
1 nutmeg grater
1 cheese grater
1 mortar and pestle

Emergency Shelf

I like to feel that I can feed an unexpected crowd within a half-hour of their arrival with a menu based on the contents of my cupboard. We like asking people back to our home after a late night's work or an afternoon in the theater. People often call and say they are in the area and can they pop around for a short visit? Over the years, I have discovered that pasta is the ideal quick meal. Everyone likes spaghetti or macaroni. While the kettle is put on to boil a great variety of sauces can be prepared within minutes, before the spaghetti has finished cooking. Cans of vegetables, mixed with olive oil and seasonings poured over freshly cooked macaroni is a simple repast. Canned fish or smoked meats will turn the simple feast into a gourmet's feast. Following is a list of basic canned and durable foods I always have on hand in the cupboard, vegetable rack or refrigerator.

Cupboard
Anchovy fillets
Tuna fish
Sardines
Canned mushrooms
Dried mushrooms
Hearts of artichokes
Jars of artichoke salad in oil
Tomato sauce[1]
Tomato purée[2]
Tomato paste[3]
Plum tomatoes
Bouillion cubes
Cans of beef and chicken consommé
Minced clams
Whole clams
Mussels
Snails
Olives
Shrimps, crab and lobster
Chicken breasts
Ham
Spinach
Peas
White kidney beans
Olive oil
Vinegar
Mayonnaise

Refrigerator
Eggs
Salami (a variety)
Prosciutto
Mortadella
Parmesan cheese
Bel Paese cheese
Salt pork
Lettuce or salad greens
Seasonal soft vegetables
Parsley
Sweet basil

Vegetable Rack
Lemons
Potatoes
Carrots
Seasonal root vegetables
Garlic cloves
Onions

Seasonings
Whole black peppercorns
Crushed red pepper
Cayenne pepper
Whole nutmeg
Paprika
Fennel seeds
Breadcrumbs
Cinnamon
Bay leaves
Oregano
Marjoram
Worcestershire sauce
Thyme
Curry powder

[1]In several countries, tomato sauce means ketchup. When I refer to tomato sauce I mean literally a sauce made from tomatoes and not the condiment.
[2]Tomato puree is a smooth blend of tomatoes.
[3]Tomato paste is often called tomato concentrate in European countries.

If, in your particular locality you do not have the precise texture of the tomato ingredient it is quite easy to blend your own from fresh or canned tomatoes.

In some areas you may not have fresh ricotta or mozzarella. Cottage cheese with little liquid can be substituted for ricotta. A soft full-fat bland cheese can be substituted for mozzarella.

I have a heavy hand with black pepper. I feel the blandness in certain dishes requires the sharpness of pepper. If $\frac{1}{4}$ cup (55 g) of black pepper to 1 lb. (454 g) ricotta seems too much for your taste buds, start with 2 teaspoons (10 g) of pepper and work upward.

How to Make Homemade Pasta

Before I begin, I must warn you of the perils that will befall you when you master the technique of making your own pasta. Your family and friends will demand it—weekly, semi-weekly, daily! Wounded, petulant expressions will appear if pasta in some form or other is not included in the menu! I have known cases where pleasant, happy personalities have turned into severe character disorders without, at the minimum, a weekly fix of this addictive dough.

Friends of ours, who are continually buying old houses, ripping them apart then adjusting the skeletons into a semblance of modernity, had suffered a rather long seige of self-inflicted discomfort with their latest purchase. Gasping for their delightful company we decided to carry lunch to them since their cooking facilities were limited to several electric fry-pans. Immediately, lasagne was requested. On a lovely summer's day we gathered in the only completed area of their home—the patio by the river—they saw their friends only in good weather. The lasagne was unfolded from its layers of insulating newspapers and foil with great tenderness. Plates were filled with warm, cheese-oozing, béchamel-brimming, basil-scented, tomato-sauced squares of pasta. A scream of horror was heard. Our friend David Baker, in a state of extreme shock ,shouted: 'Where is the spinach? I hate spinach! I only eat it when you make lasagne!' I apologized profusely; I bowed to him in supplication, tormented by the thought of loosing his friendship. I tried to enlighten him by explaining that lasagne was made in many different ways, but to this day he asks with suspicion, when being served lasagne, 'Does it have spinach at the bottom?'

Making homemade pasta is a total experience. All the warmth and joy of a friendly, happy kitchen will be yours. It is a way of life. You will put *The Waltons* to shame. I am the first to admit that I have been proselytizing all my life. Conversions have been made. I sometimes feel that my journey through life, jobs and friends is signposted by plates of spaghetti. One girl friend, who also has been combining a career and homemaking for many years, assures me that she keeps extra pans of lasagne stored in her freezer at all times, for emergencies. We appeared unexpectedly in Indiana to visit my sister for a few days and within an hour we were eating her delicious lasagne, freshly baked from the freezer.

All of you can acquire the skill necessary to make pasta. Once you have mastered the organization and techniques it takes little time to make. In fact, I have sometimes had to wait for the eight-quart kettle to come to full boil having already completed the pasta. It is a short time table: five minutes to mix, ten minutes to knead, five minutes to rest, fifteen minutes to role out and cut. The last process can be shortened to five minutes with the use of a macaroni machine.

So now that we have laid the myth of 'time-consuming' to rest I want to negate the excuse of 'no space'. Regardless of the size of your kitchen or working area you can make pasta. I have kneaded and rolled it out on some unusual surfaces; at the moment we divide our time between a *pied a terre* in London which of course has one of those postage-stamp cupboards that are euphemistically called kitchens, and a wonderfully spacious farm *cocina* in Spain. Conversely, we entertain larger groups in London where we lead a more active social life than we do in the peace and tranquility of the mountains. All you actually need is enough space to manipulate a 24-inch rolling pin and less if you use a machine. I have even rolled the dough with a glass bottle in an ill-equipped rented kitchen. My mother, who was visiting me when I shared an apartment with four other students, was horrified that I actually boiled the pasta in a pre-plastic period tin dishpan. It was the only large pot in the cupboard and I was amused at her concern, since it obviously was the cleanest pan in the kitchen. My daughter tells me that, craving spaghetti in desperation, she used a tea kettle in the dormitory kitchen! So equipment can be flexible.

Equipment

One large bread board or formica topped surface

Southern Europeans use marble surfaces which are normal fittings in their kitchens. My uncle made an excellent sturdy wooden pastry board, three feet long and two feet wide which my mother still uses after more than sixty years of wear. I use a marble slab or the wooden table in Spain, depending upon how large a quantity I am making. In the more cramped area of my London apartment I use a formica surface which is quite adequate.

Twenty-four Inch Rolling Pin

A wooden broom handle or wooden curtain dowel can be substituted. As I indicated earlier, I have used a glass bottle quite successfully.

Two Bowls

One for stirring the eggs and the other to cover the resting dough.

A Drying Area

A sheet-covered table or bed—or hang clean tea-towels over the backs of kitchen chairs. For large amounts I have strung strings over a broomstick placed between two chairs.

Ingredients

1 *lb.* (454 *g.*) *flour*
4 *or* 5 *eggs*
1 *tbsp.* (15 *ml.*) *of oil*
extra flour
water

If you wish to make a smaller amount of pasta, I usually plan on one egg more than cups of flour. Adjust the oil and water to the ratio you need. A few drops of olive oil is sufficient for 3 eggs and 2 cups (450 g) of flour. If you use too much oil it will have the reverse effect and become too malleable.

Pasta Procedure

Arrange the working surface with a sense of space and ease. All equipment should be within easy reach but far enough away not to cramp your arm and finger movements.

The wonderful moment has now arrived. Pour one pound of flour onto the work surface so that it forms a mound. With your fingers make a well in the middle of the mound. Break the eggs into a small bowl and gently stir, blending the yolk and white of the egg. Do not beat. Add one tablespoon of olive oil and one tablespoon of water to the egg mixture and stir. Many recipes tell you to use salt. I do not because it hardens the pasta, in my opinion. If you cook the pasta in plenty of salted water it will season it. Unlike the majority of recipes I use a mixture of olive oil and water because I find it makes a more supple dough. Mixing the eggs with the oil and water before you place it into the well will save time in the blending of the flour with the eggs.

Mixing

Pour the mixture of eggs and oil into the well and with your hands begin to fold the flour from the outside, over the egg mixture. Work the dough with your fingers. Be gentle but quick letting your fingers work a small amount of flour in at a time, or some of the egg mixture will find a subterranean passage and you will find yourself frantically trying to contain the liquid with your hands as it flows rapidly across the flat surface. The dough should start to stick together. You may need more water. This depends upon the quality of flour and size of your eggs. Continue to work the dough until you can form a ball from the dough.

Kneading

If you consider any of this laborious then the following ten minutes will be the most arduous. If you find it too difficult, I then beg you to give up cooking and return to convenience foods. I find kneading any dough very satisfying as a tactile and sensual experience. It becomes alive in your hands. Pat the dough with flour on your hands, into a flatter sphere. Sprinkle flour on your working surface and place the dough on it. With the heel of your hands press down and push the dough away from you. Fold the dough towards you, kneading it alternately with your right and left hand. Turn the dough clockwise as you continue the procedure. The pattern of movement will soon become rhythmic and easy to do. If the dough remains sticky sprinkle with flour. Your hands also should have a coating of flour. In about ten minutes the dough should be smooth with a silkish veneer and elastic to the touch. Do not under-knead your dough or you will have difficulty in rolling. The dough must be thoroughly blended. Instead of isometrics or wiggling about on the floor to a tuneful beat of a disgustingly cheerful radio voice at the crack of dawn exhorting you to 'Bend! Bend! Bend!' knead dough several times a week—it is excellent exercise.

Resting

Place the kneaded dough under a bowl to rest. I have not the vaguest idea why or what happens to the dough under the bowl but the outcome is worth the few minutes' wait. I usually check my sauces, prepare other ingredients or take a short stroll in the garden. When you return to the table and lift the bowl the dough will be light and elastic. Cut the dough in half. If you are going to use a machine, cut it into two inch pieces. Replace all the pieces under the bowl so they will not dry out.

Rolling by Hand

This is by far the most pleasurable. I always use this method unless I am unduly pressed for time. Sprinkle the cleaned surface with flour. Flour your rolling pin and hands. Take half of your dough and place it on the work surface. Place the rolling pin in the center and gently roll back and forth in all directions until it is flattened. Now as you roll the pin across the dough, wrap the ends around the rolling pin. Pressing down at the same time, stretch the dough sideways with your hands. It is a double movement of the wrapped dough going forwards and being stretched sideways at the same time. Turn the dough as you work and the sheet will be even. Do not use a straight forward movement that you use in rolling pastry. Keep your hands, rolling pin and emerging sheet of dough sprinkled with flour so that it will not stick as you work. Within minutes you will have a large circle of thin dough. Keep rolling until you can see the grain of the marble, wood or formica through the dough. This is pasta! The pasta, now cloth-like, will resemble a large crib sheet or bridge tablecloth. Lay it out on a clean surface to dry and roll out the other half. Let it harden for about ten minutes before cutting into the desired shapes.

The Macaroni Machine

The majority of modern machines will have a thickness gauge for the type of pasta you need. For lasagne and tagliatelle I set it at the second marking. Take a 2 inch (5 cm) piece of pasta and roll it into a tubular shape with your hands. Place it on the rollers and slowly turn until it is caught. With one hand press evenly on the dough, forcing it gently between the rollers and slowly turn the handle with your other hand. Do not rush or turn in a jerky motion as the pasta will come through looking like an enlarged slice of Swiss cheese. Once it has begun to go through the rollers evenly you can use your hand to catch the length of pasta before it folds onto the table. The pasta lengths will be approximately 2 inches (5 cm) wide. Place the dough on a cloth-covered surface to dry. The lengths can be used for lasagne or cut into other shapes. For tagliatelle or vermicelli, use the cutting attachment provided to cut more slender threads. Remember, homemade pasta takes only five minutes to cook; as soon as it rises to the top of the boiling water it is done.

Boiling the Pasta

The general rules are the same for cooking homemade pasta and commercially produced pasta. The basic method is simple: bring six to eight quarts of water to a rapid boil. Add a few drops of olive oil so that the pasta will not stick together; 1½ tablespoons (21 g) of salt is usually adequate. Always remember to salt the water. You can never remedy the error and it will taste like cooked paste.

Spaghetti

This method is suitable for all lengths of macaroni and noodles. Slip the pasta from the package into the water. Do not break the lengths of pasta. As the ends soften and begin to curl, gently stir the spaghetti with a large pronged fork until the pasta is completely immersed. I use a three-pronged fork for spaghetti. Cook for approximately ten to fifteen minutes. Check the cooking times on the packets of pasta; most commercial pasta firms research their products thoroughly in their kitchens and can advise the correct cooking times. At the approximate finishing time, lift one strand out and test it with your teeth to see if it is done. If it is, take the kettle from the fire immediately and drain. The moment between *al dente*, perfectly done pasta, to over-cooked mush is literally just one second. *Al dente* means 'just resistant to the teeth'; it is done. You do not want long strings of innocuous, bloated, pallid pasta. Do not rinse with water—the result will be cold spaghetti. Immediately put the spaghetti in a warmed serving dish or on warmed plates. If you have the odd guest as I do who is always late, return the drained pasta to the pot and cover with a tea cloth. For a large dinner party you can pre-cook the spaghetti for a few minutes, drain and re-cook in the original water and it will still be in excellent eating order. Do not worry about water not being completely drained—the spaghetti will absorb it in the bowl. For some dishes such as *Spaghetti alla Carbonara* or Summer Spaghetti you want the water and sauce to be absorbed very quickly by the strands of spaghetti. It is essential that the spaghetti is hot. I sometimes add olive oil to the pasta if the serving process is unexpectedly delayed. This will keep the noodles separated and easy to heat quickly and stir. Unfortunately, life is not utopian and therefore you must have several tricks as alternatives to perfectly served pasta.

Lasagne and Other Large Shapes

Bring the water to a boil. Add salt and a larger amount of olive oil—2 tablespoons (30 ml) should be adequate. Arrange a wet cloth on the table. Put only a minimum number of lasagne or large shapes into the pan at a time. If you place a whole packet in the pot at the same time, they will cling nauseously to each other and would be more suitable for a shoemaker than for lasagne. When the lasagne rises to the top—in about fifteen minutes—it is done. With a slotted wooden spatula lift the pasta from the water letting it drain, and place on a cloth to finish the process. If you leave the pasta in the water it will only absorb the moisture and become bloated, adding more liquid to the sauce, when added, than is necessary.

Commercial versus Homemade Pasta

Obviously, commercially made pasta is convenient, easy to store, unperishable and versatile. You should keep a large variety of types and shapes in your cupboard. I usually keep at least twenty varieties from soup pasta to baking pasta in my cupboard. Just as obviously, homemade pasta takes a bit more time to produce. For certain dishes, homemade pasta is superior to commercially made pasta—the main reason being that homemade pasta absorbs the juices of the sauce thereby enhancing the flavor. With commercial pastas, the sauce has been known to descend to the bottom of the bowl forming a miniature lake, abandoning the macaroni completely.

Serving Pasta

Pasta should be served in flat dishes with sloping sides. Some flat soup bowls will suffice but the gentle graduation of the side of the bowl should help the person manipulate the strands. I have seen all kinds of acrobatics performed with forks, knives, and spoons in the hands of the frustrated and exasperated consumer.

The Italians invented the fork, undoubtedly to tackle this gastronomic engineering problem, so use it. I remember showing off as a child, my prowess in twirling strands of spaghetti around my fork. Italian restaurants usually provide a spoon, the idea being that you twirl the spaghetti in the spoon. Nonsense! You select several strands of spaghetti with your fork, from the side of the plate nearest to you. Twirl the strands around your fork and then eat. Do not try to embarrass your mouth with a bale-like spaghetti-entwined fork so that your eyes pop from the effort. It is a delicate and restrained performance. To encourage the Neophyte, however, I must say that my husband, after twenty-one years, still cuts it in small pieces, zigzagging across the plate with a knife and fork and, with great gusto appreciatively lifts the raped spaghetti into his mouth with a spoon! However you tackle the problem, eat the pasta with pleasure.

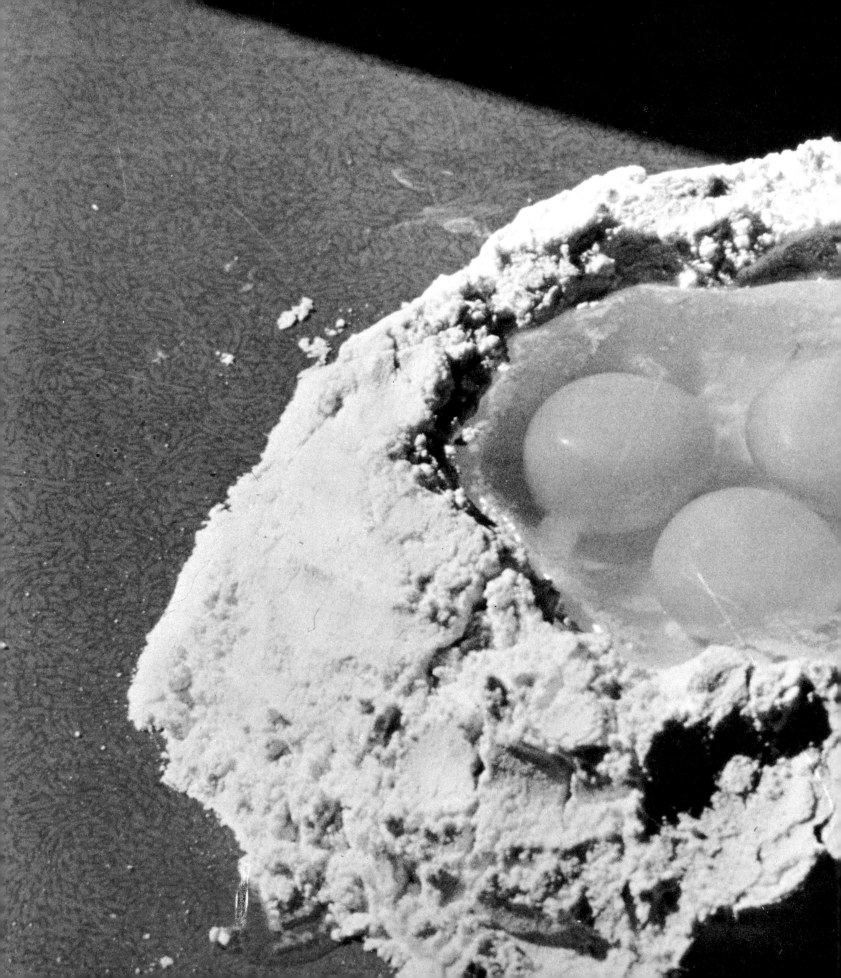

HOMEMADE
PASTA

Lasagne

Americans are most familiar with the tomato and cheese version of this perfect party dish. However, there are many variations that are delicious and appealing. I have used all of the following recipes and my guests have enjoyed them equally.

Use the key recipe for pasta dough (p. 25-28) unless I indicate otherwise.

Traditional Lasagne

Sauce:
1 (28 oz. or 780 g.) can Italian plum tomatoes
2 (6 oz. or 170 g.) cans Italian tomato paste
3 cloves garlic
1 lb. (454 g.) round steak, ground
¼ lb. (114 g.) pork, ground
4 fresh, sweet basil leaves
pinch of oregano
1 tbsp. (14 g.) chopped parsley
1 tsp. (5 g.) sugar
½ tsp. (2.5 g.) red pepper
½ tsp. (2.5 g.) black pepper, freshly ground
¼ cup (55 g.) grated parmesan cheese
salt to taste
olive oil to cover pan bottom
water

Brown the garlic in the olive oil. Add the tomato paste and stir. Pour water into the paste can and with a spoon, scrape the remaining paste to blend with the water. Add the water, plum tomatoes, basil, oregano, parsley, sugar and seasonings. In a separate pan, sauté the meat until lightly cooked. Add the meat and cheese to the mixture and stir. Bring to the boil and then simmer, stirring occasionally, for 45 minutes.

Cheeses:
1 lb. (454 g.) ricotta
1 lb. (454 g.) mozzarella
½ lb. (227 g.) grated parmesan
¼ cup (55 g.) freshly ground black pepper
½ cup (112 g.) fresh-cut parsley

Crush the ricotta in a bowl with a fork, mixing it with the black pepper and parsley. Slice the mozzarella in thin pieces. Arrange all the cheeses in front of you.

Pasta:
1 lb. (454 g.) homemade pasta cut into 3 inch (7.5 cm.) widths, 10 inches (25 cm.) long. If you insist, you may substitute ready-made pasta. I find I need 1½ packaged lbs. to equal 1 lb. of homemade pasta. Follow my instructions on cooking the pasta. Do not cook it the full cooking time because it will continue cooking in the oven. Drain the pasta on a cloth, on the table.

Assembling the Lasagne:
Arrange all the ingredients in front of you, in their order of use. Spoon ½ cup (112 g.) of tomato sauce into the bottom of an oblong baking dish. A colored ceramic dish will transfer the baked lasagne elegantly to the table, for serving. Spread the sauce about the dish. Lay approximately three lengths of pasta lengthwise in the dish. Overlap the lasagne just a bit. Place the mozzarella cheese in the approximate middle of each serving portion. Sprinkle the ricotta liberally and add the parmesan cheese more lightly. Spoon sauce to cover the layer. Arrange the next layer of lasagne across the width of the pan and repeat the arrangement of cheeses and sauce. By alternating the direction of the lasagne pattern you will ensure a compact square of cooked pasta when serving. You should have four or five layers of lasagne in the baking dish for a good serving. Bake for 45 minutes in a moderate to hot oven. It is absolutely *essential* that you let the lasagne cool for 20 minutes before you serve it; the internal temperature will ensure that it will be warm when you serve it. Lasagne must be allowed to settle before serving.

This recipe should be enough for eight portions if served as a first course, or six portions if served as the main course.

Lasagne al Forno Veronese

I often use this recipe when the normal cheeses are not available for the traditional pasta. This is a northern Italian recipe that combines a thick, creamy béchamel sauce with a tomato sauce, topped with parmesan cheese.

Pasta:
Basic lasagne recipe (1 lb. or 454 g.)

Tomato Sauce:
2 lb. fresh tomatoes, peeled, or
    1 (28 oz. or 780 g.) can Italian plum tomatoes
1 onion, chopped finely
1 tbsp. (14 g.) salt
1 tsp. (5 g.) sugar
olive oil to cover
2 tsp. (10 g.) fresh parsley
4 sweet basil leaves [2 tsp. (10 g.) dried]
2 tsp. (10 g.) ground black pepper
2 cloves garlic

Pour enough olive oil into the frying pan to cover the bottom. Add the onion and garlic and sauté until golden. Chop the tomatoes into little pieces and add to the mixture, stirring gently. When the tomatoes have become pulpy add the remaining ingredients. Simmer for 20 minutes.

Béchamel Sauce:
2 *tbsp.* (28 *g.*) *flour*
2 *tbsp.* (28 *g.*) *butter*
½ *medium onion, chopped*
1 *pint* (473 *ml.*) *milk*
½ *tsp.* (2.5 *g.*) *freshly grated nutmeg*
2 *tsp.* (10 *g.*) *black pepper*

Melt the butter in the pan and cook the onion until golden. Stir the flour into the onion butter slowly, until it begins to thicken. Add a quarter of the milk, stirring constantly. Gradually add the remainder of the milk and seasonings. Bring to the boil and then simmer for 15 minutes, stirring frequently. It is best to use a very heavy saucepan or a double boiler for a smooth sauce. You must not burn the flour or milk.

Pour a thin layer of the tomato sauce on the bottom of the dish. Lay three lengths of lasagne on the bottom of the dish and ladle the tomato sauce to cover the pasta. Pour the béchamel sauce over the tomato sauce gently so they do not mingle. Arrange the next layer in the alternate direction, adding the sauces. Continue the layering of pasta and sauces until you have used up the pasta. Sprinkle parmesan cheese and butter on top of the top layer of the lasagne. Bake for 45 minutes. Cool for 20 minutes and serve.

Lasagne and Meatballs

Pasta:
Follow basic lasagne recipe (1 lb. or 454 g.)

Sauce:
1 (28 *oz. or* 780 *g.*) *can tomatoes*
1 (6 *oz. or* 170 *g.*) *can tomato paste*
2 *cloves garlic*
4 *fresh, sweet basil leaves*
pinch of oregano
1 *tsp.* (5 *g.*) *sugar*
salt and pepper to taste
¼ *cup* (58 *ml.*) *olive oil*
water

Pour olive oil into the bottom of a heavy skillet. Cook the garlic until soft and add the paste, plus one can of water. Mix and then add the tomatoes. Using your wooden spoon, mash the tomatoes into smaller pieces. Add the seasonings and cook for half-an-hour.

Meatballs:
1 *lb.* (454 *g.*) *ground beef*
½ *lb.* (227 *g.*) *pork, ground*
½ *lb.* (227 *g.*) *veal, ground*
2 *eggs*
salt and pepper to taste
olive oil
2 *slices white bread*
½ *cup* (112 *g.*) *parmesan cheese*
1 *garlic clove, minced*
10 *parsley leaves, chopped*
pinch of crushed red pepper

Mix the meat with the seasonings in a bowl. Break the bread into crumbs and mix with the meat. Beat the eggs and cheese together and add to the meat mixture. With your hands, combine the ingredients until well blended. Take about 1 tbsp. (14 g.) of the mixture and form into small meatballs with your hands. Pour the olive oil into a skillet and brown the meatballs slowly, until cooked on all sides. Add the meatballs to the sauce and cook for another half-hour.

Cheeses:
1 *lb.* (454 *g.*) *ricotta mixed with parsley and pepper*
½ *lb.* (227 *g.*) *grated parmesan*

Assembly Procedure:
Pour only enough sauce to cover the bottom of a baking dish. Arrange the first layer of lasagne. Add the small meatballs and sauce. Spread the ricotta evenly on each layer and sprinkle lightly with parmesan cheese. Repeat the process, alternating the direction of the pasta, until you have 4 to 5 layers. Bake in a moderate oven (350°) for 45 minutes. Remove, cool till set (20 minutes) and serve.

Lasagne Verde

Pasta:
3 *cups* (330 g.) *flour*
1 *lb.* (450 g.) *fresh spinach or*
  2 *pkts. frozen, cooked and drained*
4 *eggs*

Follow the general instructions for making pasta (p. 26). After you have mixed the dough well with your hands you are ready to add the spinach. It is essential that the spinach be well-drained. Squeeze all the excess water through the colander. Add the spinach to the mixture with one or two tablespoons of the water in which you cooked the spinach. Knead the dough until the spinach, eggs and flour are completely blended. Keep your working surface and hands well floured as the dough has a tendency to be sticky. Divide the dough into two or three pieces. Roll the dough out on a floured board with a well-floured rolling pin. Cut the sheet into 3 inch (7.5 cm.) lengths and dry for 20 minutes. Cook in rapidly boiling, salted, oiled water for 5 minutes and drain onto a tea cloth.

Sauce:
Follow the recipe for traditional lasagne (p. 32) except use Italian Sausage (1 lb. or 454 g.) instead of the ground meat.

Cheeses:
1 *lb.* (454 g.) *ricotta, mixed with*
½ *cup* (112 g.) *parsley and*
¼ *cup* (55 g.) *freshly ground black pepper*
½ *lb.* (227 g.) *grated parmesan cheese*

Assemble the lasagne in alternating layers, covering each layer with the sauce and cheeses. Bake in a moderate oven (350°) for 45 minutes. Cool, set and serve.

Lasagne Verde
Meatball sauce is a useful variation on this popular party theme.

Lasagne with Sausage

Follow the recipe for Meatball Sauce (p. 33) except substitute 2 lb. (908 g.) Italian sausage for the meatballs. Cut the Italian sausage into 1 inch (2.5 cm.) lengths, sauté in skillet until cooked. Drain the sausage on absorbent paper and add the sausage to the sauce. Assemble the lasagne, with the cheeses and sauce, in the same manner as the key recipe (p. 32).

Lasagne and Ham Mornay

Pasta:
Follow basic recipe (1 lb. or 454 g.)

Sauce:
1 *pt.* (473 *ml.*) *bechamel sauce* (*p.33*)
2 *egg yolks, beaten*
½ *cup* (112 *g.*) *grated parmesan or gruyere cheese*
2 *tbsp.* (28 *g.*) *butter*

Bring the béchamel sauce to a boil. Add the beaten yolks and butter to the sauce and lower the heat to a simmer. When blended add the cheese. Cook till the cheese has melted.

Ham:
Thin slices of Baked Ham (½ lb. or 227 g.). Use a subtle ham, not overly salty. Virginia or Polish ham work quite well with this dish.

Pour a thin layer of the sauce on the bottom of a rectangular baking dish. Arrange the pasta in the bottom of the pan. Cover the pasta with the béchamel sauce. Arrange the thin slices of ham to cover the sauce. Repeat the pattern, alternating until you have five layers. Sprinkle parmesan cheese over the top layer, grind some black peppercorns over the top and bake for 45 minutes in medium oven (350°). Cool, set and serve with a garnish of watercress or fresh parsley.

Lasagne with Cauliflower

1 *pint* (473 *ml.*) *mornay sauce*
½ *lb.* (227 *g.*) *sliced gruyere (Swiss) cheese*
1 *large cauliflower, cooked and broken into florets*
ground black pepper
1 *lb.* (454 *g.*) *lasagne*
butter

Cook the pasta in the traditional way and drain on a tea cloth. Heat the mornay sauce. Drain the cauliflower carefully. The flowers should be cut into small pieces, not mashed but small enough to make a smooth layer. Arrange the pasta in a rectangular baking dish in alternating layers with a cover of mornay sauce, cauliflower and sliced cheese. Cover the top layer with the remaining sauce, dot with butter. Sprinkle freshly ground pepper over the top and bake for 45 minutes in a moderate (350°) oven. Cool, set and serve garnished with tomato wedges.

Leona's Party Lasagne

Pasta:
2 *lb.* (908 *g.*) *homemade lasagne cooked and drained*

Meat Sauce:
2 *pints* (950 *ml.*) *meat sauce (use double the basic meat sauce—*
  (*p.* 139)

Cheeses:
2 *lb.* (908 *g.*) *ricotta mixed with ½ cup* (112 *g.*) *ground black*
  pepper
2 *lb.* (908 *g.*) *mozzarella* (5 *little mozzarella buds*) *sliced*
1 *lb.* (454 *g.*) *freshly ground parmesan cheese*

Spinach:
2 *lb.* (908 *g.*) *fresh spinach, cooked and drained*
black pepper
freshly ground nutmeg

Béchamel Sauce:
2 *pints* (950 *ml.*) *béchamel sauce* (*p.* 33)

Arrange the cheeses, sauce and pasta in a row in front of
you. Spread the cooked spinach with your fingers across the
bottom of the baking dish. I usually use two rectangular
ceramic baking dishes and fill them both at the same time—
a bit like an assembly line. Grate nutmeg over the spinach.
It should be subtle, not overwhelming so five or six twists
will do it. Grind black peppercorns evenly over the spinach.
Sprinkle the ricotta liberally on the layer and add the slices
of mozzarella cheese. Sprinkle the parmesan cheese lightly.
Spoon the meat sauce over the cheese and then the béchamel
sauce. Continue this procedure: pasta, cheeses and sauces,
alternating the layers as you progress. Five layers should
make a sizeable lasagne. Bake in a moderate (350°) oven
45 minutes. I usually place aluminum foil on the bottom of
the oven to catch any exuberant juices that might boil over
the side. Cool the pasta for 20 minutes which will set it
nicely and make it much easier to serve.

For a first course, this is sufficient for 16 to 18 servings—
you will always have the dear lady who is dieting. It should
serve 16 comfortably for a main course. This is an ideal dish
for a buffet supper.

Leona's Party Lasagne
Popular with people of all ages, this standby has always
been an unlimited success.

38

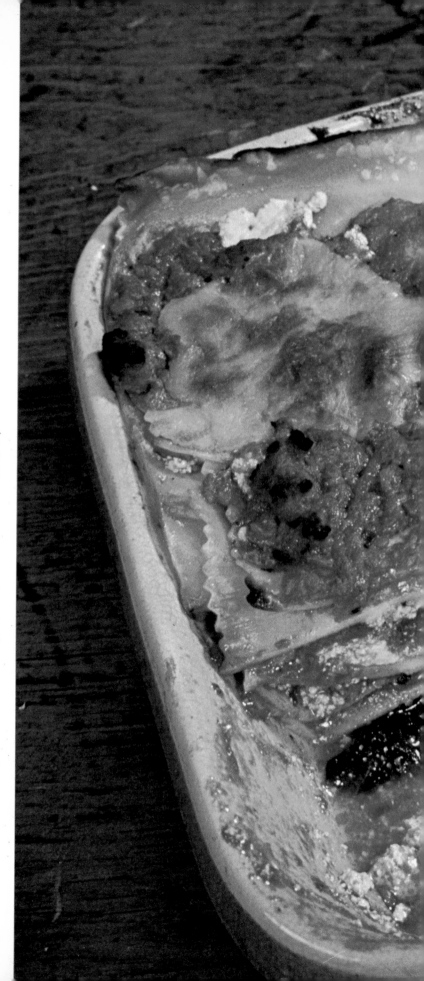

Ravioli

These small, stuffed squares of pasta are very familiar to most of you, covered with a tomato sauce. However, the variety of fillings and sauce combinations are endless. Try mixing them in a variety of combinations. Below I mention a few of the fillings and sauces. We co-ordinate, mix and match everything—from towels to wallpaper, so create combinations that will be your very own.

Basic Ravioli Dough

2 *cups* (450 *g.*) *sifted flour*
3 *egg yolks, beaten*
1 *egg, beaten*
¼ *tsp.* (2 *g.*) *salt*
7 *tbsp.* (100 *ml.*) (*approx.*) *warm water*

Make a well in the flour on a pastry board. Beat the egg, egg yolks and salt together. Mix the dough with fingers, working the egg and flour together. Add the water as you need it. Blend the dough till it is smooth. Form the dough into a ball. Let it rest for 15 minutes. Place the dough on a well-floured board. Knead the dough for 10 minutes till it is smooth and elastic. Brush the ball of dough with olive oil and replace under the bowl for 10 minutes. Divide the dough into two uneven parts. Roll the smaller piece until very thin on a well-floured board. Heap 1 tsp. (5 g.) of the filling, approximately 2 inches (5 cm.) apart, in straight rows, on one sheet of pasta. There are ravioli forms and carved rolling pins available but with a good eye you can evenly space the filling on the sheet. Fold the other sheet of dough over the bottom, starting at one end. The top sheet should be larger and will mould itself around the mounds of filling, as you bring the remainder of the pastry forward. With your fingers, gently arrange the dough more firmly around the filling. Cut along each row of fillings with a pastry cutter. Then cut between each mound, leaving little stuffed pillows. Press a fork lightly around each edge, sealing the ravioli. Cook in plenty of salted, boiling water until they rise to the top. Serve immediately.

Stuffings

Ricotta Ravioli

1 *lb.* (454 *g.*) *ricotta cheese*
¼ *cup* (55 *g.*) *parsley, freshly chopped*
2 *eggs*
2 *tbsp.* (28 *g.*) *grated parmesan cheese*
salt to taste
black pepper
1 *tbsp.* (14 *g.*) *flour*

Mix the ricotta cheese with the parsley, parmesan cheese, salt and black pepper. Beat the eggs and add the flour, slowly, to the mixture. Combine the egg and flour with the cheese mixture. Place a tsp. (5 g.) of filling for one ravioli. Excellent with meat sauce, served plain with butter and parmesan cheese or cooked in chicken broth for a first course.

Beef Stuffing

½ *lb.* (227 *g.*) *minced beef*
1 *egg, beaten*
½ *onion, grated*
½ *slice white bread*
2 *tbsp.* (30 *ml.*) *white wine*
½ *tsp.* (2.5 *g.*) *marjoram*
¼ *cup* (55 *g.*) *freshly cut parsley*
¼ *cup* (58 *ml.*) *olive oil*
salt and pepper to taste
¼ *cup* (55 *g.*) *parmesan cheese*

Sauté the onion until soft in the olive oil. Break the bread into crumbs and add. Cook the minced beef lightly with bread, wine and onion. Take from the stove and cool. Add the herbs, cheese and beaten egg. Mix well and place 1 tsp. (5 g.) of the mixture for one ravioli. Serve with a simple tomato sauce or cooked in bouillion, served with butter and parmesan cheese.

Spinach and Meat Stuffing

½ lb. (227 g.) ground beef or veal
1 cup (225 g.) parmesan cheese
1 lb. (454 g.) fresh spinach
olive oil
3 eggs
black pepper
nutmeg
salt to taste

Sauté the ground meat lightly in a heavy skillet. Steam the spinach in salted water for only 2 minutes. Remove and drain. Beat the eggs and add the beef, cheese, spinach, nutmeg and black pepper to the mixture. Mix well.

A meat sauce—Ragu—is an excellent combination.

Spinach and Cheese Stuffing

Use the same recipe as above but substitute 1 lb. (454 g.) ricotta cheese for the meat. You may want to use a bit more black pepper. Serve with a thin béchemel sauce or soured cream.

Brains, Liver and Veal Stuffing

1 set of brains, blanched and veined (½ lb. or 250 g.)
5 pairs chicken livers
½ lb. (227 g.) cooked, minced veal
2 eggs, beaten
olive oil
1 tbsp. (15 ml.) brandy
2 tsp. (10 g.) nutmeg
¼ cup (55 g.) parsley
¼ cup (55 g.) black pepper
pinch of thyme
½ onion, chopped
salt to taste

Mash the blanched brains and minced veal. Sauté the onion until soft and add the chicken livers. Remove from the heat and add the brandy, eggs, seasonings, brains and veal. Mix well. Make the ravioli. Cook the ravioli in a hearty chicken stock. Remove the ravioli, thicken the broth with 1 cup (240 ml.) of cream and pour over the ravioli.

Chicken and Mushroom Stuffing

1 onion, chopped
1 cup (225 g.) cooked, diced chicken
½ lb. (227 g.) fresh mushrooms, sliced
1 slice of bread, soaked in
2 tbsp. (30 ml.) wine
2 tsp. (10 g.) parsley
black pepper
salt to taste
2 eggs, beaten
olive oil to cover

Pour olive oil to cover the bottom of a pan. Sauté the onion until soft and add the sliced mushrooms. In a bowl, break up the bread. Add wine. Stir in the eggs and seasoning. Add chicken, onion and mushrooms. Stir well.

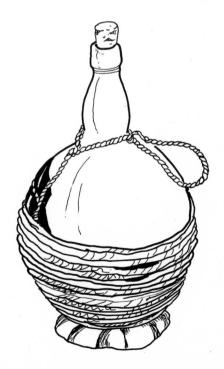

Cannelloni

My personal preference for a special pasta treat is a dish of béchamel-covered, stuffed cannelloni. I like party dishes which can be prepared hours ahead of time. Add the sauce to the prepared cannelloni and bake. Within a half an hour you have an elegant dish fit for the most discerning gourmand. My knowledge of cannelloni came late in life—I was first served these delicate stuffed pasta on a bed of spinach by Mrs. Bird in her charming flat in Greenwich Village. She and her late husband, General Ivor Bird, for many years assigned to British Embassies as an Air Attache, adored Italy and its cuisine. She usually served cannelloni on her birthday in his memory: a sentimentality I appreciated. Since that time I have roamed about the Continent especially northern Italy and Spain. I discovered the incredible versatility of—as one restaurant in La Hucana, Spain, translates as 'little icicles'—these delicate stuffed rounds of pasta. The traditional Italian cannelloni is stuffed with lamb. I have used venison with equal success.

Dough

Use the basic pasta recipe. After rolling the dough into thin sheets, cut the pasta into 4 inch by 4 inch (10 cm. by 10cm.) squares. You can buy ready-made tubes but somehow the thickness of the pasta dough overwhelms the filling.

Traditional Cannelloni

1 lb. (454 g.) pasta dough cut into squares, cooked and drained.

Stuffing:
¾ lb. (340 g.) minced lamb or venison
½ onion
2 tsp. (10 g.) nutmeg
1 tsp. (5 g.) black pepper, ground
salt and pepper to taste
2 tsp. (5 ml.) béchamel sauce (optional)*
½ cup (112 g.) parmesan cheese
2 tsp. (10 g.) chopped parsley
2 eggs
olive oil

Sauté the onion in the olive oil until soft. Add the minced lamb/venison. Cook for 5 minutes. Beat the eggs and add the remaining ingredients. Combine with the meat and onion.

    *I find it makes a creamier filling if you mix two teaspoons of the béchamel sauce with the filling.

Sauce:
1 pint (473 ml.) béchamel sauce, made with
1 cup (237 ml.) chicken broth and
1 cup (237 ml.) of milk
[I usually add 1 tbsp. (14 g.) of parmesan cheese, grated.]

Lay the pasta square flat. With a teaspoon, arrange about one tablespoon of filling along one edge of the square. Do not over fill. Roll the pasta into a tube. Arrange the cannelloni in a rectangular dish or small ceramic individual serving dishes. Three cannelloni make a good first course and four, if it is the main course. Cover the cannelloni with the sauce and sprinkle parmesan cheese over the top. Dot with butter and bake in a hot (400°) oven until brown on top or place under a grill until brown and bubbling.

Party Cannelloni

I double the above recipe, adding ½ cup (112 g.) of sliced mushrooms and arrange the cannelloni on a bed of well-drained, freshly cooked spinach. Remember that the two seasonings that enhance pasta dishes are nutmeg and freshly ground black pepper. Be liberal with both.

Meat Stuffed Ravioli
A rich tomato and meat sauce is the perfect compliment to these delicate stuffed pillows.

Cannelloni in Catalonia

One of the customs in Spanish Catalonia is to drive on Sunday with your family to one of the hundreds of small family-run restaurants that grace every town, hamlet or crossroads, for lunch. I think that, second only to a picnic and mushrooms in the mountains, these charming parties exemplify the Spaniards' love of food and family. The groups usually include not only the parents and children but the grandparents, sisters and brothers, all their children plus the odd godparent or two. They converge on the selected restaurant in four or five cars, laughing and talking —the women busily arranging the children into immediate chaos, the men lingering amongst the trees until the table is ready for their lunch. The meals are extended three-hour, multi-coursed triumphs of excellent food, wine and company. Eating out in a restaurant crosses all economic and social barriers. It is not just financially well-endowed people; farmers, salesmen and professionals mingle in a variety of inns that range from an obscure, simple ten to twelve table restaurant to large converted farm houses whose rooms ramble through a maze of doorways and stone steps. Country restaurants have small playgrounds which quite cleverly occupy the children and therefore keep the family happy. The menus vary from seafood, game, meat and sausages grilled on the open fire or cooked slowly with subtle sauces. Always on the list is the Sunday Special— Cannelloni. The fillings vary from region to region—bit more rabbit here, heavier use of liver and gizzard there, or perhaps a delicate chicken and veal stuffing with herbs. The sauce! How a plain, white sauce can absorb the sophisticated nuances and slight innuendos of a familiar but not quite definable herb or seasoning, is baffling. My husband and I considered it our duty to plunge forward into the hinterlands, away from the more popular, rather tourist-oriented restaurant to discover how many different fillings and sauces were available to us for Sunday lunch. Neither gout nor fear of calories kept us from this pleasant quest. Unfortunately it would take the better part of a year to accomplish this task fully and we have only visited fifty or so in our area.

Below are some of the most distinctively delicious recipes we found.

Pau Xich Restaurant

Make the normal pasta dough. Roll out into a thin sheet and cut into 3 inch by 4 inch rectangles. Cook until *al dente* in plenty of salted water and drain. Place on a wet towel until you are ready to use.

Filling:

¼ *lb.* (114 *g.*) *loin pork, minced*
¼ *lb.* (114 *g.*) *minced chicken* (*legs or thighs*)
6 *chicken livers, cut in pieces* (6 *oz.* or 170 *g.*)
¼ *lb.* (114 *g.*) *sausage* (*use breakfast sausage meat*)
1 *brain* (¼ *lb.* or 114 *g.*)
1 *minced onion*
2 *minced tomatoes*
2 *tbsp.* (30 *ml.*) *oil*
2 *tsp.* (10 *ml.*) *anisette*
2 *tsp.* (10 *ml.*) *brandy*
1 *tsp.* (5 *ml.*) *water*

In a frying pan sauté the pork, chicken, chicken livers and sausage meat in olive oil till brown. Parboil the brain. Remove the outer membrane. Cut into small pieces and add to the meat mixture. Cook for 10 minutes. Add the onion, tomatoes, anisette, brandy and water. Stir until the mixture is blended.

Sauce:

4 *cups* (950 *ml.*) *milk*
3 *tbsp.* (42 *g.*) *flour*
1 *tsp.* (5 *g.*) *salt*
3 *tbsp.* (42 *g.*) *butter*
2 *egg yolks, beaten*

Melt the butter in a frying pan and blend in the flour. Stir in the milk slowly, until the sauce is smooth. Add the egg yolks and salt. Cook until thickened.

Place one tablespoon (15 grams) of the stuffing on each cannelloni and roll it into a tube. Place four cannelloni in individual oven-proof dishes, cover with béchamel sauce and sprinkle with red pepper, butter and grated cheese. Bake until brown on top.

Jaume Ventura, Pau Xich Restaurant,
Guardiola de Fontrubi (*Barcelona*)

Hostal Domingo Restaurant

Prepare the dough as in previous recipe. Cut shapes, cook and drain onto a wet cloth.

Filling:
3 oz. (85 g.) pork loin, minced
3 oz. (85 g.) beef, minced
2 oz. (55 g.) pork liver
1 brain
4 tbsp. (55 g.) butter
¼ cup (58 ml.) olive oil
3 medium onions, minced
2 tbsp. (28 g.) breadcrumbs
4 tbsp. (55 g.) flour
salt to taste
2 tbsp. (30 ml.) brandy
½ cup (118 ml.) wine
1 egg yolk

In a frying pan, sauté the meat separately. Parboil the brain, remove membrane and fry. All meats should be well-cooked. Remove the last of the meats and fry the onion until brown. Mix the milk, salt, flour, breadcrumbs and brandy with the meat. Put in a warm oven (300°) and bake for one hour. Remove. Put ½ cup of béchamel sauce with the mixture, stir in the egg yolk and wine.

Sauce:
1 quart (946 ml.) milk
4 tbsp. (55 g.) butter
4 tbsp. (55 g.) flour
1 tsp. (5 g.) cinnamon
1 tsp. (5 g.) salt

Melt the butter and stir in the flour. Stir in the milk and stir until smooth. Add the seasonings and cook for 20 minutes.
Fill the cannelloni and roll into a tube. Arrange on a heated baking dish. Cover with the sauce, sprinkle with cheese and butter. Bake for 10 to 15 minutes, or until brown.

Jesus Carriou, Domingo,
Villafranca de Penedes (Barcelona)

Hostal Mateau

The same recipe as above, except one tomato is chopped into the sauce with ½ tsp. (2½ g.) hot pepper.

Hostal Mateau, La Llunuca (Barcelona)

Senora Carmen Carol

My dear friend, Carmen, makes cannelloni frequently in her home for her extended family. We have enjoyed many meals and fiestas (from the Feast of the Three Kings to the 'Killing of the Pig') with the Carols who are extremely generous with their hospitality.

Pasta:
As basic recipe

Filling:
2 chicken hearts
½ lb. (227 g.) veal
½ lb. (227 g.) pork loin
3 chicken livers
1 sausage (4 oz./114 g.)
¼ cup (58 ml.) olive oil
2 tsp. (10 g.) cinnamon
1 onion, minced
2 tomatoes

Put a small amount of oil into a saucepan. Cook the meat till well-done (half-an-hour). Remove from the fire. Drain the meat but keep the juices in the pan. Add the onion, cinnamon and tomatoes. Cook until soft and blended. Remove from the fire. Mince when cool.

Sauce:
In the saucepan mix: 3 tbsp. (42 g.) of flour with the juices in the frying pan. Add one quart (946 ml.) of milk, 1 tsp. (5 g.) salt and cook until thick. Stuff the cannelloni and place in a buttered casserole. Strain the sauce over the cannelloni. Sprinkle with cheese and butter. Grill for 10 minutes.

Guardiola (Barcelona)

Pork Sausage and Sweetbreads Stuffing

1 *onion, chopped*
¼ *cup* (58 *ml.*) *olive oil*
nutmeg
black pepper
pinch of thyme
½ *lb.* (227 *g.*) *pork sausage*
½ *lb.* (227 *g.*) *sweetbreads*
¼ *cup* (55 *g.*) *parmesan cheese*
4 *oz.* (120 *ml.*) *white wine*
2 *eggs*

Cook the onion until translucent. Remove the sausage from the skins and lightly cook in the same oil. Blanch the sweetbreads and add to the pork sausage. Cover with wine and cook until the wine evaporates. Remove. Crush the meat with a fork until minced. Add the eggs, cheese, onion, and seasonings to the meat mixture. Place one tablespoon (about 15 g.) of the filling on each cannelloni square. Roll and place in a rectangular oven dish. Cover with a béchamel sauce. Bake in a hot (400°) oven until brown on top. Serve immediately.

Beet Top and Cheese Stuffing

½ *lb.* (227 *g.*) *ricotta cheese*
½ *lb.* (227 *g.*) *beet tops or spinach*
1 *tsp.* (5 *g.*) *black pepper*
¼ *cup* (55 *g.*) *parmesan cheese*
pinch of nutmeg
1 *egg, beaten*
salt to taste

Crush the ricotta in a bowl. Parboil the beet tops until just soft, in salted water. Chop into small pieces and add to the ricotta. Mix. Add the egg, parmesan cheese and seasonings. Mix well. Place one tablespoon of the filling on each cannelloni square and roll it into a tubular shape. Cover with a béchamel sauce and bake in a hot (400°) oven until brown on top. Serve immediately.

Spinach-Stuffed Cannelloni
Nutmeg scented béchamel sauce covers the stuffed tubes of egg pasta—a perfect blend of flavors.

46

Fuselli

This is a traditional pasta dish served during Easter week. I am grateful to my buttonhole Aunt, Mary Brindisi of Utica, New York for this recipe.

Dough:
Basic dough

Break the dough into small pieces and roll pencil thin, like a shoe string. Break into 3 inch (75 mm.) pieces and roll around a slender iron wire with your fingers until the whole wire is covered. Slip the fuselli or spindles off the iron wire and dry on a towel. If you are not near an area where they sell Italian cooking utensils you can use a wire from an umbrella frame or a long, thin knitting needle. The wire should be approximately 12 inches (30.5 cm.) long. Cook the fuselli in rapidly boiling salted water, drain and serve with a breadcrumb sauce.

Sauce:
2 *cups* (450 g.) *fresh breadcrumbs*
1½ *cups* (340 g.) *pine nuts* (*you can substitute almonds*)
3 *tbsp.* (42 g.) *olive oil*
salt and pepper to taste

Place your breadcrumbs into a hot, heavy skillet. Stir constantly until they are brown. Add the pine nuts and olive oil and blend evenly. As soon as the nuts are hot, pour over the strained fuselli and serve.

Fuselli can also be served *al burro* (with butter and parmesan cheese) or with one of your favorite sauces.

See page 52 for a color illustration of this tempting dish.

Fettuccine
Fettuccine al Burro

This simple noodle dish called fettuccine in Rome and tagliatelle in other areas has become an epicurean classic.

Basic Dough:
1 lb. (454 g.)

Roll your dough into thin sheets and let it dry. Be sure it is well-floured. Roll like a jelly roll and cut ¼-inch (64 mm.) slices from the dough. Sprinkle with corn meal if you are not going to use them immediately. Boil the noodles in well-salted water for 5 minutes. Remove with a slotted spoon and place in a heated serving dish. Toss the noodles with one cup (225 g.) of soft butter. Serve at once with parmesan cheese.

Fettuccine Alfredo

This recipe has become known as *Fettuccine al Alfredo*— named after the owner of the restaurant in Rome who created the original recipe—homemade noodles tossed with butter and cheese. Along the way, cream was added to the butter and cheese which makes the dish less authentic because the Italians use very little cream in their sauces or dishes. If you do not use homemade noodles then the cream will help make a richer sauce.

Basic Noodle Dough:
Cut in ¼ inch (64 mm.) strips and boil until *al dente*. Drain the noodles and place on a platter in a warm oven.

Sauce:
Combine the hot noodles with 1 cup (225 g.) butter and 1 cup (225 g.) parmesan cheese. Quickly toss and serve. I usually add 5 or 6 twists of the pepper grinder. Serve with additional cheese. The secret is to have a very hot serving dish so that the butter and cheese melt quickly. You can pop the serving dish into a warm oven to blend the cheese and butter.

Slices of ham or proscuitto blend well with this dish to make it a heartier meal.

Fettuccine Alfredo
Homemade noodles tossed in butter and freshly grated cheese is a simple but elegant dish.

Tortellini

Tortellini al Burro (Little Hats)

This recipe is a step away from ravioli but much less filling and is used because of its charming shape. Tradition has it that it was inspired by a woman's navel.

Roll the basic dough into a flat sheet. Cut into 2 inch (5 cm.) squares. Place $\frac{1}{4}$ to $\frac{1}{2}$ teaspoon (1 to 2 g.) of the filling into the center of the square. Fold one corner towards the other forming a triangle. Fold the double corner and bring back. Pinch the ends of the dough and wrap the tube around your finger forming a little halo-shaped hat. Place on a towel and dry thoroughly—1 to $1\frac{1}{2}$ hours.

Cook in well-salted water until they rise to the top. Remove with a slotted spoon to a towel to drain and serve immediately with butter and cheese, or a meat sauce, depending upon the filling.

Meat Filling:
1 cup (225 g.) cooked chicken or veal minced
$\frac{1}{2}$ cup (112 g.) parmesan cheese, grated
1 tsp. (5 g.) nutmeg
2 eggs, beaten
salt to taste
1 cup (225 g.) ricotta
1 cup (225 g.) drained cooked spinach
2 tsp. (10 g.) freshly ground pepper

Combine the eggs, cheeses and seasoning. Add the meat and mix well. Excellent with a ragu sauce or in a beef broth.

Cheese Filling:
2 cups (450 g.) ricotta
$\frac{1}{2}$ cup (112 g.) chopped parsley
$\frac{1}{2}$ cup (112 g.) parmesan cheese
pinch of nutmeg
2 eggs, beaten
2 tsp. (10 g.) black pepper
salt to taste

Combine the cheeses with the beaten eggs and add the seasonings. Mix well. Serve hot with butter and cheese or a light tomato sauce.

Tortellini Timbale

Some years ago an English national Sunday paper, at the time of England's entrance to the EEC, ran a contest for the best European amateur cook. Much to everyone's surprise and my joy, a wonderful, plump nanny from Italy won the contest hands down, with her version of a macaroni timbale. This is my recipe for a superb dish that takes a bit more time to make but is well worth the effort. It sounds heavy—a pasta-filled pie—but let me assure you it is as light as a feather. Make the pastry dough first, so that it can chill while you are preparing the remainder of the dish.

Pasta:
Arrange the dough into little squares ready for stuffing.

Stuffing:
$\frac{1}{2}$ cup (112 g.) chopped veal, minced
$\frac{1}{2}$ cup (112 g.) chopped chicken giblets
$\frac{1}{2}$ cup (112 g.) minced sweetbreads (can use chicken)
1 onion
olive oil
2 eggs, beaten
pinch of thyme and rosemary
$\frac{1}{2}$ cup (118 ml.) brandy
$\frac{1}{4}$ cup (55 g.) chopped parsley
2 cloves garlic

Fry the onion and garlic until soft. Remove from heat and add the chicken livers and giblets and cook for 10 minutes. Add the brandy and continue cooking until the liquor has evaporated. Remove from the heat and add the seasonings and eggs. Mix until well blended. Stuff the seasoning into tortellini shapes.

Gravy:
1 cup (118 ml.) chicken bouillon
1 carrot
1 onion
1 turnip
$\frac{1}{2}$ lb. (227 g.) mushrooms, sliced
1 cup (237 ml.) thin ragu
$\frac{1}{2}$ cup (118 ml.) white wine
nutmeg
salt and pepper
2 tbsp. (28 g.) flour
2 tbsp. (28 g.) butter
1 tbsp. (14 g.) tomato concentrate

Cook the carrot, onion and turnip in the bouillon until soft Blend the butter and flour in another pan and gradually add to the broth until thickened. Add seasonings and blend well. If you wish a smoother gravy, use your blender. I prefer a pithy content to the gravy.

Pastry Dough:
3 cups (675 g.) flour
1 cup (225 g.) sugar
2 tsp. (10 g.) grated lemon rind
3 egg yolks
1½ cups (340 g.) butter

Blend the butter and flour together. Add egg yolks, sugar and lemon rind. Let it set for an hour or place in the refrigerator for one-half hour.

Assembly:
Roll out two-thirds of the pastry to a very thin crust. Line a well-greased deep casserole. In a large bowl, combine the cooked tortellini and gravy. Pour into the pastry shell. Roll out the remaining dough and cover the casserole. Decorate the top with pastry leaves and flowers. Brush with egg white. Cook in a medium hot (375°) oven for 45 minutes or until brown on top and the sides are pulling away from the dish.

Gnocchi

We raced home from school on the days that the buttonhole Aunt, Margaret Flint, visited us because we knew she would be making her special blend of soft shell-shaped gnocchi for lunch. The following is her recipe.

Wash, pare and cook three medium-sized potatoes in salted water for about 20 minutes or till tender. Drain. Dry the potatoes by shaking the pan over the fire. Mash the potatoes and keep hot. Measure 1¾ cups (400 g.) sifted flour. Make a well in the flour and add the hot mashed potatoes. Mix well to make a soft elastic dough. Turn dough onto a floured board and knead until elastic. Break off small pieces of dough and using the palm of your hand, roll the pieces to pencil thickness. Cut into pieces about ¾ inch (2 cm.) long. Curl each piece by pressing with index finger and pulling the finger along the piece of dough towards you. Boil rapidly in salted water, uncovered, for 10 minutes or until they rise to the surface. Drain and serve with parmesan cheese and meat sauce.

A richer potato gnocchi can be made by adding an egg yolk to the above recipe. They are very good if you place the gnocchi in a fireproof casserole, cover with parmesan cheese and butter and bake in a hot oven until brown. Gnocchi also blend well with a chicken liver sauce.

Spinach Gnocchi

The Italians dearly love spinach blended with, or complementary to, their pasta dishes. This is a superb luncheon dish that has great subtlety and flavor.

1 lb. (454 g.) spinach, cooked
½ lb. (227 g.) ricotta cheese
2 oz. (55 g.) parmesan cheese
pinch nutmeg
1 tsp. (5 g.) butter
2 eggs
3 tbsp. (42 g.) flour
salt
1 tsp. (5 g.) pepper

Chop the well-drained (almost dry) spinach. Place the spinach with the seasonings, ricotta cheese and butter in a bowl. Stir till blended—5 to 6 minutes. Beat the eggs, flour and parmesan cheese together. Add to the mixture. It is best if you make this the night before and keep it well covered in the refrigerator. Flour a pastry board and with your hands pinch about one tablespoon (15 g.) of dough and roll into a tubular shape of about 2 inches (5 cm.) long. Roll in flour and cook in rapidly boiling salted water. As soon as they bounce to the top take them out with a slotted spoon and drain. Place in a buttered baking dish, cover with parmesan cheese and butter. Put the dish into a warm oven until the cheese is soft. Serve hot.

Fuselli Al Burro (*overleaf*)
Delicate twists of egg pasta tossed with butter and parmesan cheese make an excellent accompaniment to meat—roasted or grilled.

COMMERCIAL PASTA

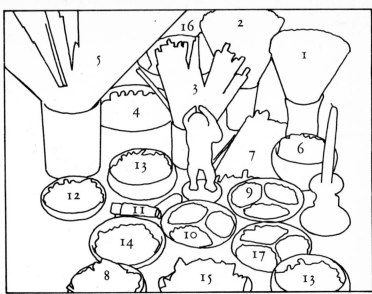

A sample of the many types of commercially produced pasta that I have used in the preparation of the recipes for this book.

1. Whole-wheat spaghetti
2. Linguine
3. Zitoni
4. Conchiglia
5. Spaghetti
6. Rigatoni
7. Lasagnette and flat spaghetti
8. Tagliatelle or Fettuccine
9. Pastina
10. Pastina
11. Cannelloni
12. Ziti
13. Fuselli
14. Ditali
15. Farfalle
16. Lasagne Verde
17. Miscellaneous Small Pasta Shapes

As children, my father told us many stories. Usually they were the librettos of Italian operas that he eloquently dramatized with wonderful expressions of pain and joy. How we cried with Pagliacci! I was twelve before I realized that operas could possibly be written by someone other than Verdi or Puccini.

One of my favorite stories was the tale he told of his mother when she was newly married. My grandfather was coming home on leave from one of the many wars that preoccupied Italy in the late 19th century. Grandmother wanted to do something very special for the homecoming. A wonderful idea came to her head and she set out on foot for the larger village near their home. She purchased a packet of commercially made spaghetti from a shop and began her return journey home. She passed several women sitting on chairs in front of their doorways and they cried out, 'Eh, what is that you have?' Grandmother had shoved the long, blue-wrapped roll under her apron to avoid being questioned by just such gossips. 'We see your belly sticking out! Mama mia, what a miracle! And your husband away so long!' Gleefully they approached her and tugged at her apron until the loosely tied bundle of spaghetti dropped onto the ground. The long strings of pasta scattered like a grand game of pick-up-sticks. She was mortified! The women taunted her: 'Too lazy to make your own, eh?' She burst into tears, gathered up the now dusty spaghetti and said, 'It was a surprise for my Luigi! He comes home today!' As she retreated along the street towards her home they followed her, laughing and teasing along the way.

What, then, is the difference between commercially made pasta and *pasta fatta in casa* (pasta made in the home)? It is a difference in texture and quantity of design. I refuse to say 'convenience'. Pasta is quite simple to make! Pasta, commercial or homemade, is mixed with water. Homemade pasta usually is made with eggs as the binding agent and little water. Commercial pasta with the exception of egg noodles (Fettuccine or Tagliatti or Tagliatelle) is made from pure semolina durum wheat and water. The quality of the water has a good deal to do with the taste and texture of pasta. The water should be soft. The best pasta in Italy is from the Naples area because the local water supply has the proper softness with which a delicate pasta can be made.

As a child I wandered along the shelves of the Italian store where we purchased most of our groceries, looking at the ends of the pasta packets. The small drawing depicting the name, size and number of the pasta intrigued me; all the curly macaroni, the little bows, the huge ribs of rigatoni and the fairytale quality of all the little soup pastinas. These fanciful shapes were fed to us quite early in life. I must say I enjoyed being ill as a child. It was great fun to be coddled and to participate in the routine of illness. We were tenderly placed in our parents' huge bed as soon as the cold, or the first measle spot appeared. You slunk securely down into the starched sheets and pulled the soft blankets up close to your chin. Lunch would arrive on a pale green bed tray covered with a white doily. And there would be the little bowl of pastina! Tiny stars, wheels, rice-shaped, or minute lengths of macaroni with the smallest hole that only a thread could pass through, were the variety from which Mama selected. Depending upon the illness, the pastina would be in chicken broth or mixed with a heartier egg, and butter. Whatever the mixture the pastina would slide down gently, warmly caressing the stomach. A perfect food.

The variety of commercial pasta known to most Americans is limited. We lump pasta into two general headings: spaghetti and macaroni. This is erroneous; the words 'macaroni' and 'pasta' are interchangeable. Spaghetti is a form of macaroni or pasta whichever word you choose to use. The most thin, long strand of pasta is capellini. The largest holed, long strand is ziti (zitoni). The widest length of flat, long pasta is lasagne. The most narrow, flat pasta is linguine.

Following is a complete list of pasta that you can buy in America.

Pasta

Soup Pastinas

(*cooking time:* 7-10 *minutes*)
1. Conchigliette, or chinesini (little shells)
2. Annellini
3. Nochette
4. Acini de Pepe
5. Semini di Melo

Long Pasta Strands

1. Tagliatelle
2. Tagliatelle verde (spinach noodles)
3. Fuselli
4. Spaghettini
5. Spaghetti
6. Ziti
7. Mezzani
8. Lasagnette
9. Linguine—flat shaped spaghetti
10. Zitoni—large tubular pasta
11. Lasagne—flat and curly
12. Lasagne verde (with spinach:

Short Thick Shapes of Pasta

(*cooking time:* 10-14 *minutes*)
1. Pennini—short tubes cut at an angle
2. Occhi di Lupi—larger smooth tubes of macaroni
3. Penni—larger holed, angle-cut short spaghetti
4. Elbow macaroni
5. Grosso Rigato—small ribbed tube shape
6. Conchiglia—small conch-shaped shell
7. Farfalle—large butterfly shapes
8. Cravattine—smaller cravat shape
9. Ruote—cog wheel shape
10. Tortiglioni—short twists
11. Cappelletti—little hats

Pasta for Stuffing

(*cooking time:* 15-20 *minutes*)
1. Rigatoni—ribbed tube
2. Manicotti—smooth large tube
3. Cannelloni—large round tubes, sometimes ribbed or sold in squares to be rolled
4. Lumache—large conch-shell shape
5. Ravioli—small squares
6. Tortellini—naval shaped
7. Agnolotti—half circles

Some of the names I have mentioned are interchangeable, depending on the manufacturer or on the part of the country. Some names have been anglicized. I know 'Pennini', for instance, is just referred to as short-cut macaroni. Rather than harass your local grocer, I suggest you buy visually. Obviously if you are going to stuff a large shape you will visually see that manicotti or rigatoni are such shapes. You should incorporate the Italian's love and flair for using the wide variety of shapes. Pasta shapes have been given such loving, affectionate names by the Italians—butterflies, little cocked hats, kisses, angel's breath, cravats to name but a few. In my recipes I will suggest various shapes that can be used but for heaven's sake, do not accept my word as gospel. I am constantly experimenting and interchanging pastas in dishes. Use your imagination and with some selectivity you can achieve an excellent pasta vocabulary.

The manufacture of pasta is based on the earliest methods used by the Italian housewife. In some parts of Italy they still make spaghetti by hand through an enlarged wire strung frame called a *chitarra*. 'Chitarra' means 'guitar'. The cook rolls her pin over a wide strip of pasta placed on the frame. What emerge are long, thin strands of spaghetti. The principle then is to force the dough through a form and press out the desired shape. In the home, spaghetti is dried over a clean cloth-draped chair or across poles in the open air in the sun. The modern process, of course, uses all the advantages of technology in hygenic conditions. The wheat is ground into a course meal. The bran is removed and this product is called semolina. The sifted meal is mixed with hot water in huge vats and thoroughly kneaded to a smooth, stiff dough. It is then placed into a steam-jacketed metal cylinder. The end of the cylinder has a die fitted to it in one of the many varieties of pasta shapes. The dough is pressed through the die by a plunger or press which forces the pasta through the holes. The tubular shapes are hung to dry over wooden rods in a drying oven where they will be gently caressed by currents of warm air. Only authentic pasta will bear its own weight in drying.

There is a wonderful story about spaghetti and spring madness. Some years ago, a major television network in England ended its News summary with an announcement that they would now go over to their correspondent in Italy where the spaghetti trees were in bloom. The picture on the television screen was of a lovely panorama of the Italian countryside. The correspondent was standing in a grove of trees. The camera zoomed in on the announcer and he commented that the Italian country-side was ablaze with the fruits of spring. The camera panned across the orchard and there were the trees with long strands of spaghetti hanging from their boughs, softly bending with the wind. The next day the television network was inundated with letters and calls asking if they could be planted locally; where could they buy the plants and what conditions were necessary for breeding? Only a very few twitted the television company about their succumbing to spring fantasies! As Barnum said: 'There's one (fool) born every minute'.

Following are recipes that use commercially made pasta.

Simple Skillet Meals (Cheese and Egg)

The following pasta recipes take from 10 to 30 minutes to prepare in a skillet. The dishes are ideally suited to being a first course, luncheon, or a light supper if accompanied by a salad and dessert. Remember to follow the general instructions for cooking pasta *al dente*. The majority of the sauces can be made while the pasta is cooking.

Spaghetti al Burro

1 *lb.* (454 *g.*) *spaghetti*
¼ *cup* (55 *g.*) *black pepper*
1 *cup* (225 *g.*) *butter*

Boil the spaghetti in rapidly boiling, salted water until *al dente*. In a skillet, melt the butter. Drain the spaghetti into the skillet. Add the black pepper. Toss quickly with two large forks so that all the spaghetti is covered. Serve immediately with parmesan cheese.

German Noodles with Toasted Breadcrumbs

4 *tbsp.* (55 *g.*) *butter*
1 *cup* (225 *g.*) *breadcrumbs*
½ *lb.* (227 *g.*) *noodles*
parsley

Cook the noodles until *al dente*. Toss lightly with butter, breadcrumbs and parsley.

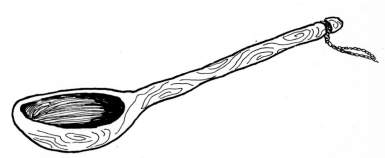

Noodles with Butter, Cheese and Parsley

1 *lb*. (454 *g*.) *noodles*
½ *cup* (112 *g*.) *parmesan cheese*
½ *cup* (112 *g*.) *mozzarella cheese*
½ *cup* (112 *g*.) *butter*
¼ *cup* (55 *g*.) *chopped fresh parsley*
salt and pepper

Boil the spaghetti in rapidly boiling, salted water until *al dente*. In a skillet, melt the butter, cheese and parsley. Drain the noodles immediately and add to the skillet. Twist a pepper grinder 5 or 6 times over the top and toss quickly with two large forks. Serve immediately.

Spaghetti with Black Pepper and Nutmeg

1 *lb*. (454 *g*.) *spaghettini*
1 *tsp*. (5 *g*.) *nutmeg*
¼ *cup* (55 *g*.) *black pepper, freshly ground*
¼ *cup* (58 *g*.) *olive oil*

Cook the spaghettini until *al dente* in rapidly boiling, salted water. Drain. Remove to a warm serving dish and add the olive oil, nutmeg and pepper. Toss quickly with two forks until the spaghettini is well covered. Serve with grated parmesan cheese.

Spaghetti Omelette

(A good way to use left-over spaghetti)

2 *cups* (450 *g*.) *cooked spaghetti*
black pepper
salt
¼ *cup* (55 *g*.) *parmesan cheese*
1 *onion, chopped*
4 *eggs*
¼ *cup* (55 *g*.) *chopped parsley*
½ *cup* (118 *ml*.) *olive oil*

Beat the eggs with the salt and pepper. Add the onion, parsley, cheese and spaghetti. In an omelette pan or rounded skillet, pour enough olive oil to cover the bottom of the pan. Heat it until a drop of water sizzles. Pour your egg and spaghetti mixture into the pan. Lower the heat and cook until brown on the bottom. Turn the omelette over and cook until brown. Remove from heat and serve immediately.

Spaghetti with Black Pepper and Nutmeg
Try this for lunch with a green salad and a light dry wine.

Spinach Noodles with Herb and Cheese Sauce

1 *lb.* (454 *g.*) *spinach noodles*
3 *tbsp.* (42 *g.*) *butter*
3 *tbsp.* (42 *g.*) *flour*
2 *cups* (450 *g.*) *milk*
3 *egg yolks, beaten*
¼ *cup* (55 *g.*) *chopped parsley*
2 *tsp.* (10 *g.*) *dried basil leaves*
2 *tsp.* (10 *g.*) *oregano*
½ *tsp.* (2.5 *g.*) *salt*
2 *tsp.* (10 *g.*) *pepper*
1 *lb.* (454 *g.*) *ricotta*
½ *lb.* (227 *g.*) *mozzarella*
½ *lb.* (227 *g.*) *cream cheese*
pinch cayenne pepper

Melt butter and add flour, blending until thick. Gradually add the milk until the sauce begins to bubble. Stir in the egg yolks, seasonings and cheeses. Cook until the cheeses have melted. Cook the noodles until *al dente*. Mix the sauce and the macaroni until the noodles have begun to absorb the sauce. Serve garnished with cayenne pepper.

Linguine with Egg

1 *lb.* (454 *g.*) *linguine (narrow, flat noodles)*
1 *cup* (225 *g.*) *butter*
4 *eggs, beaten*
½ *cup* (112 *g.*) *parmesan cheese*

Boil the linguine until *al dente*. Heat the butter and cheese in a skillet. Drain the pasta and put it immediately into the skillet and add the beaten eggs. Toss quickly over a low flame until the egg is cooked. Serve hot with parmesan cheese.

Noodles with Ricotta

1 *lb.* (454 *g.*) *wide noodles*
½ *lb.* (227 *g.*) *ricotta*
salt
½ *cup* (112 *g.*) *butter*
½ *cup* (112 *g.*) *parmesan cheese*
¼ *cup* (55 *g.*) *parsley, chopped*
⅛ *cup* (28 *g.*) *black pepper*

Mix ricotta, black pepper and chopped parsley in a bowl. Cook the noodles in rapidly boiling, salted water. Melt the butter in a skillet. Add the cheeses, and stir gently. Drain the noodles and mix with the cheeses, stirring constantly. Serve hot with additional parmesan.

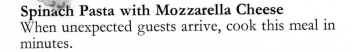

Spinach Pasta with Mozzarella Cheese
When unexpected guests arrive, cook this meal in minutes.

Spaghetti with Olive Oil and Garlic

1 *lb.* (454 *g.*) *spaghetti*
½ *cup* (118 *ml.*) *olive oil*
salt and pepper
6 *cloves garlic*

Mince the garlic into small pieces. Heat the olive oil and gently cook the garlic until it is soft. Cook the spaghetti in boiling salted water—drain. Arrange on a warm dish and pour the olive oil and garlic mixture over the top. Mix with a fork and serve.

Noodles with Olive Oil and Cheese

Substitute 1 lb. (454 g.) of noodles in the above recipe. Add: ½ cup (112 g.) parmesan cheese to the noodles and sauce. Toss until the noodles are well-covered.

Macaroni with Mozzarella

1 *lb.* (454 *g.*) *heavy, short macaroni* (*ziti, rigatoni*)
½ *lb.* (227 *g.*) *mozzarella, in cubes*
¼ *cup* (55 *g.*) *parsley*
½ *cup* (118 *ml.*) *olive oil*
6 *cloves garlic, crushed*
black pepper
salt

Cook the macaroni until *al dente*. In a skillet, brown the garlic in the olive oil. Add the mozzarella cheese. Remove from heat. Drain the macaroni well. Place in a heated serving dish, pour the olive oil and cheese mixture over the top, add the parsley and seasonings and mix well. Serve with parmesan cheese.

Egg Pastina

This recipe is quite often served as an invalid dish. My family like it anytime, it is so delicious. Choose one of the tiny pastina shapes.

½ *lb.* (227 *g.*) *pastina*
½ *cup* (112 *g.*) *butter*
2 *eggs,* *beaten*
black pepper

Boil the pastina in rapidly boiling, salted water. They do not take long—only about 6 minutes. Drain in a strainer and pour into a heated bowl. Add the butter and 2 eggs quickly. Toss into the bowl. With a spoon, mix quickly as the heat of the pastina will cook the egg. Serve hot, with parmesan cheese on the side.

Egg Pastina
A delicate dish for the sick child but a favorite between illnesses as well.

VEGETABLES

The following recipes are especially suited to the summer season when our larders burst with new grown vegetables and herbs: plump tomatoes, sweet onions, zucchini, cabbages, broccoli, the noble pepper and whatever the heart fancies. With today's skill of freezing, summertime can be anytime and even city dwellers have easy shopping access to the frozen vegetable. With a good wine, cheese and crusty bread, these pasta dishes are perfect for the hot weather appetite.

Spaghetti with Pisto Sauce

1 *lb*. (454 *g*.) *vermicelli*
1 *bunch fresh sweet basil*
3 *cloves garlic*
2 *oz*. (60 *ml*.) *olive oil*
3 *tbsp*. (42 *g*.) *pine nuts*
$\frac{1}{3}$ *cup* (75 *g*.) *grated parmesan cheese*
1 *tsp*. (5 *g*.) *salt*

Remove the basil leaves from the stems and cut into small pieces. Mince the garlic and the pine nuts. Combine the three in a mortar with salt. Pound until the mixture is puréed. (You can use a blender for this.) Add cheese. When the mixture is soft, slowly add the olive oil and stir. When the mixture has taken all the olive oil, it should have a thick, creamy consistency. Cook the vermicelli in boiling salted water till *al dente*. Drain and place in warm dishes. Spoon a few tablespoonfuls of the 'pisto' over the top of the hot vermicelli.

This dish originated in Genoa where they do not use parmesan cheese but a much stronger cheese, pecorine. Pecorine is not usually available outside our larger cities but generally, parmesan or romano cheese is easily obtainable. If you do not grow sweet basil in your garden or window box and it is not available locally, fresh parsley can be substituted, but it obviously will have a different taste. Walnuts can be substituted if pine nuts are not available. With all these substitutions you have a different but equally delicious sauce.

Spaghettini with Pine Nuts

1 *lb*. (454 *g*.) *spaghettini*
$\frac{1}{2}$ *cup* (118 *ml*.) *olive oil*
2 *cloves garlic, crushed*
$\frac{1}{4}$ *cup* (55 *g*.) *fresh parsley, chopped*
salt and pepper
$\frac{1}{2}$ *cup* (112 *g*.) *pine nuts*

Cook the spaghettini in boiling salted water. In a skillet, cook the minced garlic in the olive oil until soft. Do not burn. Drain the spaghettini into a warm serving dish and add the olive oil, pine nuts, garlic, chopped parsley and black pepper. Toss quickly until the pasta is well-coated and serve.

Ditali with Walnuts

1 *lb*. (454 *g*.) *ditali or other short-cut macaroni*
$\frac{1}{2}$ *cup* (118 *ml*.) *olive oil*
2 *cloves garlic, minced*
2 *tsp*. (10 *g*.) *parsley*
$\frac{1}{2}$ *cup* (112 *g*.) *chopped walnuts*
$\frac{1}{2}$ *cup* (112 *g*.) *ricotta cheese*
2 *tsp*. (10 *g*.) *black pepper*
$\frac{1}{2}$ *cup* (118 *ml*.) *white wine*

Cook the ditali until crunchy. Pour the olive oil into a skillet and add the garlic, ricotta cheese and wine. Stir until the ricotta is creamy. Add the black pepper and parsley. Drain the ditali and add to the skillet mixture. Stir well until the pasta is covered. Serve on heated plates.

Rigatoni, Eggplant and Bacon

1 lb. (454 g.) rigatoni
1 medium eggplant (aubergine)
1 clove garlic, minced
2 tsp. (10 g.) minced parsley
½ cup (58 g.) olive oil
4 slices thick-cut bacon, chopped
3 fresh tomatoes
salt and pepper
1 small green pepper, sliced
1 cup (240 ml.) white wine
pinch red pepper

Cook the garlic in the olive oil until brown. Add the pieces of bacon and slowly cook. Skin and cut the tomatoes. Slice the eggplant and then chop into small pieces. Soak the eggplant in cold, salted water. Cut the pepper into small pieces. Add the tomatoes, pepper and seasonings to the olive oil. Drain the eggplant and add to the above mixture. Add the wine, cooking furiously until the sauce has reduced—about 5 minutes. Cook the rigatoni until *al dente* and drain. Pour the sauce over the rigatoni until blended. Serve hot.

Spaghetti and Tomatoes

1 lb. (454 g.) spaghetti
5 large, ripe tomatoes
4 sprigs of parsley
1 tsp. (5 g.) salt
5 basil leaves
1 clove garlic, minced
pinch hot pepper
¼ cup (58 ml.) olive oil

Drop the tomatoes into boiling water to remove skin. Pour the olive oil and garlic into a large skillet. Add the skinned tomatoes, breaking them up with a wooden spoon. Add the parsley, salt, basil leaves and hot pepper. Stir and cook gently for 5 minutes. Do not mash the tomatoes into a smooth sauce. Cook the spaghetti in salted, boiling water and drain. Pour the tomato mixture over the spaghetti in a warm dish. Toss quickly and serve with parmesan cheese.

Spaghetti with Fennel and Mushrooms

2 *large fresh fennel bulbs*
$\frac{1}{4}$ *cup (58 ml.) olive oil*
$\frac{1}{4}$ *cup (55 g.) butter*
1 *lb. (454 g.) spaghetti*
$\frac{1}{2}$ *lb. (227 g.) sliced mushrooms*
2 *tsp. (10 g.) parsley*
1 *clove garlic*
$\frac{1}{2}$ *cup (120 ml.) white wine*
salt and pepper

Parboil the fennel until a knife goes into the bulb, but with resistance. Do not fully cook. In a skillet, sauté the garlic in the olive oil and butter until mushy. Cut the fennel (including the stems and fern) into small pieces and sauté in the pan. Add the sliced mushrooms, white wine and seasonings. Cook the spaghetti until *al dente* and drain. Add the spaghetti to the skillet and quickly stir until the pasta is covered. Serve hot with parmesan cheese.

Noodles with Fennel and Mushrooms
Fennel with the haunting flavor of anisette braised in butter and wine is a taste treat.

Spaghetti and Artichoke Hearts

1 *large tin of artichoke hearts, sliced*
½ *cup* (118 *ml.*) *olive oil*
½ *tsp.* (2.5 *g.*) *hot, red pepper, crushed*
1 *tsp.* (5 *g.*) *salt*
1 *lb.* (454 *g.*) *spaghetti*
2 *tbsp.* (28 *g.*) *fresh parsley*
2 *cloves garlic, minced*
black pepper
parmesan cheese
3 *black olives, minced*
juice of 1 *lemon*

In a saucepan, combine the artichokes, olive oil, pepper, salt and garlic. Stir until hot. Add the parsley and lemon juice. Cook the spaghetti until *al dente* and drain. Toss the spaghetti with the sauce and serve hot with parmesan cheese. Garnish with the minced black olives.

Spaghetti with Mushrooms

½ *lb.* (227 *g.*) *mushrooms*
1 *lb.* (454 *g.*) *spaghetti*
1 *clove garlic*
2 *tbsp.* (28 *g.*) *parsley*
¼ *cup* (56 *g.*) *butter*
1 *onion, minced*
2 *tomatoes, chopped*
½ *cup* (118 *ml.*) *beef stock*
salt and pepper
¼ *cup* (58 *ml.*) *olive oil*

Clean and slice the mushrooms. Heat the butter and olive oil. Brown the garlic and remove. Cook the mushrooms until just tender. Remove. Add the beef stock, onion and chopped tomatoes to the skillet. Cook until blended and the stock is slightly reduced. Return the mushrooms to the skillet. Cook the spaghetti in salted, boiling water. Drain and mix with mushroom sauce. Garnish with the parsley and serve hot with parmesan cheese.

Artichoke Hearts with Egg Noodles
A quick cupboard meal that has a distinctive taste.

Pasta Andalucia

1 *lb.* 454 g.) *spaghetti twists*
6 *lb.* (2.72 *kg.) tomatoes*
2 *small green peppers*
1 *onion*
1 *quart* (950 *ml.) chicken broth*
1 *cup* (237 *ml.) water*
¼ *cup* (58 *ml.) olive oil*
1 *tsp.* (5 *g.) salt*
½ *tsp.* (2.5 *g.) pepper*
1 *clove garlic*

Clean, skin and chop the tomatoes. Cut the green peppers into strips; chop the onion and garlic and in a deep frying pan (2 quarts or 2 liters) sauté the garlic and onions in the olive oil. Add the tomatoes and peppers. Sauté for 5 minutes. Pour the chicken broth, salt, pepper and 1 cup water into the skillet. Bring to a boil, add the spaghetti twists and return to a full boil. Then lower the heat until it simmers gently. Cook for 14 minutes or till the spaghetti is *al dente*. Serve on heated plates and sprinkle liberally with parmesan cheese.

Pasta Andalucia
Spaghetti twists with a quick summer sauce of peppers and tomatoes.

Farfalle and Cauliflower

1 large cauliflower
1 lb. (454 g.) farfalle (butterflies)
½ cup (112 g.) butter
¼ cup (58 ml.) olive oil
salt and pepper
parsley
1 clove garlic

Break the cauliflower into small buds. Parboil the cauliflower. In a skillet, cook the garlic in the olive oil/butter mixture, until brown. Remove. Add the cooked cauliflower and seasonings. Cook the farfalle until chewy; drain and mix with the cauliflower sauce. Serve hot with a good portion of parmesan cheese.

Macaroni and Cabbage

1 small head cabbage (savoy is particularly good)
½ cup (118 ml.) olive oil
½ onion, minced
1 tbsp. (14 g.) tomato purée
1 cup (240 ml.) chicken broth
black pepper
salt
1 tbsp. (14 g.) flour
1 clove garlic
1 tsp. (5 g.) fennel
1 lb. (454 g.) macaroni

Cut the cabbage into slices. Cook the cabbage in the chicken broth until well done. Remove the cabbage but save the broth. In a saucepan, sauté the garlic and remove. Add the onion, cooking until golden. Add the tomato purée and seasonings. Gradually add 2 tbsp. (30 ml.) chicken broth to the flour until a smooth paste is formed. Add the remaining chicken broth, stirring continuously. Add the broth to the saucepan and cook until the sauce is thickened. Add the cabbage. Cook the macaroni until al dente. Mix the cabbage sauce and the macaroni together. Serve hot.

Rigatoni and Broccoli

1 lb. (454 g.) fresh broccoli
¼ cup (55 g.) butter
¼ cup (58 ml.) olive oil
2 cloves garlic
1 lb. (454 g.) rigatoni
1 tsp. (5 g.) nutmeg
salt and pepper
1 tbsp. (15 ml.) lemon juice

Separate the broccoli into florets and steam in just enough water to cover. Add 1 tsp. (15 g.) salt at the end, to retain the green color. Melt the butter in the olive oil. Sauté 2 cloves garlic until brown. Remove. Add the broccoli to the mixture adding 1 tsp. (5 g.) ground pepper and the lemon juice. Cook the rigatoni in boiling salted water until tender but not mushy. You can use part of the broccoli water if you like a well-flavored macaroni. Drain the rigatoni and add it to the broccoli mixture. Stir gently, not breaking the macaroni until the sauce is completely mixed. Serve hot, with parmesan cheese.

Rigatoni Stuffed with Spinach

1 lb. (454 g.) rigatoni
1 lb. (454 g.) cooked, drained spinach (or beet tops if available)
1 tsp. (5 g.) nutmeg
2 tsp. (10 g.) black pepper
½ tsp. (2.5 g.) salt
½ cup (120 ml.) white wine
¼ cup (55 g.) butter
2 cloves garlic
1 cup (225 g.) ricotta
1 egg, beaten
parmesan cheese

Cut the garlic into small pieces. In a bowl, combine the cheese, spinach, egg and seasonings. Cook the rigatoni until tender. Dry carefully and stuff the tubes with the spinach and cheese mixture. Lay in a greased, oven-proof casserole and pour ½ cup (120 ml.) white wine over the tubes. Dot with butter and parmesan cheese. Place under the grill until the butter has melted. Serve.

Vegetable Market (right)

Macaroni with Mixed Summer Vegetables

1 lb. (454 g.) short-cut, tubular macaroni
3 ripe tomatoes
1 pepper
1 small zucchini
¼ cup (58 ml.) olive oil
5 sweet basil leaves
1 tsp. (5 g.) black pepper
1 cup (225 g.) mushrooms
2 onions
½ cup (112 g.) green beans
1 tsp. (2.5 g.) salt
½ cup (120 ml.) white wine
1 clove garlic
1 tsp. (5 g.) oregano
½ tsp. (2.5 g.) red pepper

Wash mushrooms and slice. Blanch and peel the tomatoes. Cut the onion into slices, ¼ inch (64 mm.) thick. Break the green beans into 1 inch (2.5 cm.) lengths. Slice the zucchini. Sauté the garlic and onions in the olive oil until translucent. Add the vegetables, seasonings and wine. Simmer for 15 minutes until the vegetables are cooked but not mushy. They should be crunchy to the teeth. Boil the macaroni in salted boiling water till cooked *al dente*. Drain. Remove to a warm serving dish and pour the sauce over the top. Sprinkle generously with romano cheese and serve.

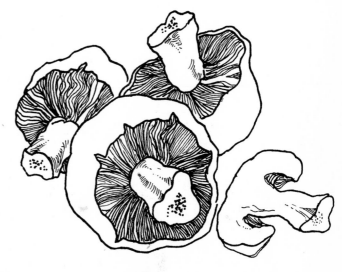

Noodles with Summer Vegetables
Straight from your garden to create a quick sauce with a summer's flavor.

81

Green Noodles with Onions and Mushrooms

1 lb. (454 g.) green noodles
¼ cup (55 g.) butter
¼ cup (58 ml.) olive oil
½ lb. (227 g.) mushrooms
4 large onions
1 tsp. (5 g.) black pepper
½ tsp. (2.5 g.) marjoram
½ tsp. (2.5 g.) salt
½ cup (118 ml.) white wine
1 tbsp. (14 g.) cornflour

Wash and slice the mushrooms. Peel and slice the onions in ¼ inch (64 mm.) lengths. Sauté the onions and mushrooms in the olive oil/butter mixture. Stir so they do not burn or brown. Add the seasonings. Mix the cornflour in the wine until dissolved. When the onions are golden add the wine. Turn the heat up and stir quickly until the mixture thickens. Lower the heat and simmer for 5 minutes. Cook the green noodles in boiling, salted water, drain and turn the noodles into the skillet, tossing the mixture quickly. Serve with a slice of mozzarella cheese on top (Bel Paese can be substituted).

Spaghetti Alla Pizzaiola

1 lb. (454 g.) spaghetti
1 tsp. (5 g.) salt
5 garlic cloves
3 sprigs chopped parsley
2 lb. (908 g.) ripe tomatoes
¼ cup (58 ml.) olive oil
2 tsp. (10 g.) oregano
1 tsp. (5 g.) black pepper

In a large skillet, sauté the garlic cloves until soft. Blanch and peel the tomatoes. Cut into wedges and add to the olive oil. Cook until the tomatoes become soft but not mushy. Add the seasonings, simmer for 3 minutes. Cook the spaghetti in salted boiling water, drain into a warm dish and pour the sauce over the top. Sprinkle generously with parmesan cheese and serve.

Spaghetti with Zucchini

1 lb. (454 g.) spaghetti
2 ripe tomatoes
1 large zucchini
½ tsp. (2.5 g.) hot red pepper
½ tsp. (2.5 g.) fennel seeds
1 onion
½ cup (120 ml.) red wine
½ tsp. (2.5 g.) salt
¼ cup (58 ml.) olive oil

Chop the onion and sauté in the olive oil. Blanch and peel the tomatoes and cut into chunks. Slice the zucchini in thin slices. Add the tomatoes, zucchini, seasonings and wine into the skillet. Cook the spaghetti until al dente. Drain and add to the skillet; stir and lift the spaghetti with a fork until it is well-covered. Serve with parmesan cheese.

Noodles with Tomato and Breadcrumbs

1 lb. (454 g.) wide noodles
1 cup (225 g.) pine nuts or walnuts
½ cup (110 g.) parmesan cheese
1 cup (225 g.) fresh breadcrumbs
2 cloves garlic
4 tbsp. (60 ml.) olive oil
4 plump tomatoes, skinned
2 sprigs parsley
4 sweet basil leaves
salt and pepper

In a skillet, lightly sauté the tomatoes, garlic and seasonings, in the olive oil. In another skillet, brown 1 cup (225 g.) of breadcrumbs until toasted. Add the nuts, cheese and about 4 tbsp. (60 ml.) olive oil. Blend. Cook the noodles until al dente. Drain and arrange on a heated platter. Spoon the tomato sauce over the top and then sprinkle the breadcrumb mixture. Serve hot with parmesan cheese.

Pasta with Peas

1 *cup* (240 *ml.*) *chicken broth*
¼ *cup* (58 *ml.*) *olive oil*
½ *chopped onion*
2 *tbsp.* (30 *ml.*) *Italian tomato paste*
½ *cup* (120 *ml.*) *wine*
¾ *lb.* (340 *g.*) *short-cut macaroni*
½ *tsp.* (2.5 *g.*) *salt*
1 *tsp.* (5 *g.*) *black pepper*
1 *tsp.* (5 *g.*) *oregano*
½ *lb.* (227 *g.*) *peas*

Sauté the onion in the olive oil until golden. Add the tomato paste, chicken broth and wine, stirring till blended. Add the seasonings and peas. Cook for 10 minutes until the liquid has been reduced. Cook the macaroni until tender but not mushy. Mix the sauce with the cooked macaroni. Serve hot, with parmesan cheese.

Noodles with Black Olives and Herbs

16 *large, pitted black olives, sliced*
¼ *cup* (55 *g.*) *freshly grated black pepper*
½ *cup* (112 *g.*) *parmesan cheese*
1 *lb.* (454 *g.*) *noodles*
2 *tsp.* (10 *g.*) *mixed Italian seasoning* (*oregano, basil, thyme*)
½ *cup* (118 *ml.*) *olive oil*
½ *tsp.* (2.5 *g.*) *hot pepper*
2 *tbsp.* (28 *g.*) *capers*

Combine in a bowl the olives, pepper, cheese, seasonings and olive oil. Cook the noodles until *al dente*. Drain and immediately mix with the olive mixture until the noodles are well covered. Serve hot with additional parmesan cheese.

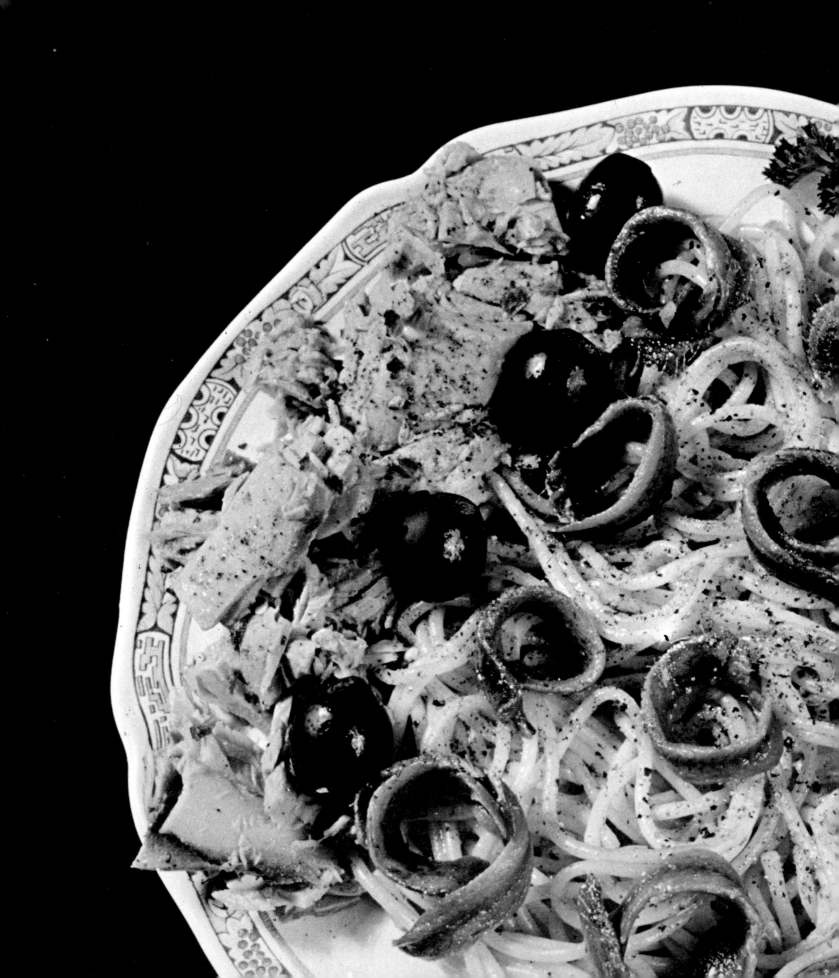

FISH

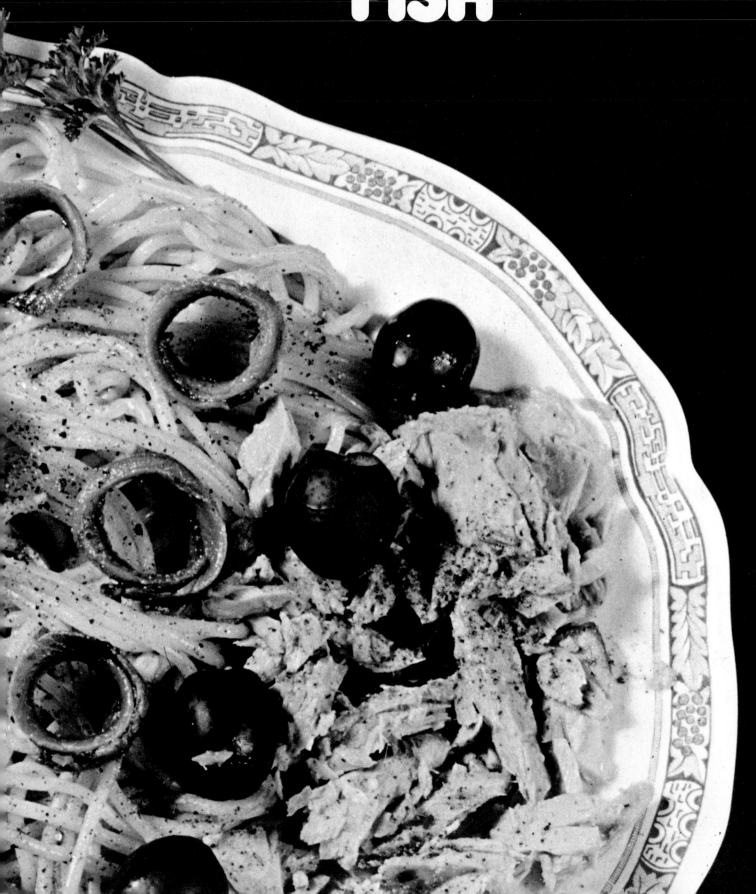

If you are lucky enough to live near the sea or a lake and have fresh fish available to you, consider yourself very fortunate. As a child, fish was something to be gulped grudgingly on Fridays, during Lent and on Christmas Eve. An exotic lobster or plump Gulf shrimp were the only true delights in childhood-seafood gourmandizing. What a limited point of view! The Japanese have long known the value of fish in the diet. Tiny slivers of raw fish with a piquant sauce, boiled fish on skewers with a sweet crispy flavor and of course noodles, cooked with a broth and small bits of vegetables and fish. Any of you who have been in the Orient are familiar with the noodle shops and the tinkling bell of the noodle man making his nocturnal way through the streets tempting people from bed to indulge in a hot, steaming bowl of noodles. The Mediterranean countries also use fish as a daily diet but usually deep fried, stewed or grilled. The lowly salt cod emerges as a succulent edible combined with any number of sauces. Even if fresh fish is not accessible, you have available to you excellent canned fish that make instant meals, combined with pasta.

Following is a variety of recipes that I have tempted my family and friends into eating to overcome their Anglo-Saxon prejudice for meat and potatoes.

Vermicelli with Anchovies and Garlic

1 *lb.* (454 *g.*) *vermicelli*
10 *to* 15 *anchovy fillets* (2 *cans*)
6 *cloves garlic, chopped*
½ *cup* (118 *ml.*) *olive oil*
¼ *cup* (58 *ml.*) *olive oil*
2 *tsp.* (10 *g.*) *black pepper*
1 *tsp.* (5 *g.*) *chopped parsley*
¼ *cup* (55 *g.*) *parmesan cheese*
¼ *cup* (55 *g.*) *fresh breadcrumbs*

Sauté the garlic in ½ cup (118 ml.) olive oil until soft. Add the anchovies but try not to mash them. Stir gently with a fork. Add the pepper and parsley. Cook the vermicelli until *al dente*, in boiling salted water. Drain and add to the skillet, tossing the pasta until it is well covered. Serve with parmesan cheese mixed with toasted breadcrumbs and olive oil.

Spaghetti and Tuna Fish

1 *lb.* (454 *g.*) *thin spaghetti*
2 (6 *oz.* or 170 *g.*) *cans tuna fish*
10 *black, pitted olives*
¼ *cup* (55 *g.*) *chopped parsley*
4 *cloves garlic, minced*
2 *tsp.* (10 *g.*) *freshly ground pepper*
½ *cup* (118 *ml.*) *olive oil*

Sauté the garlic in olive oil until brown. Cook the spaghetti in salted water until *al dente* and drain into a warm serving dish. Pour the olive oil, garlic, parsley, black olives, black pepper over the mixture. Toss thoroughly until the pasta begins to absorb the oil. Arrange the tuna fish over the top and serve.

Noodles with Tomato and Tuna Fish

1 *lb.* (454 *g.*) *noodles*
2 (6 *oz.* or 170 *g.*) *cans tuna fish*
2 *cloves garlic*
1 (28 *oz.* or 780 *g.*) *can tomatoes*
½ *minced onion*
½ *tsp.* (2.5 *g.*) *oregano*
1 *tsp.* (5 *g.*) *sweet basil* (4 *fresh leaves*)
2 *tsp.* (10 *g.*) *chopped parsley*
½ *tsp.* (2.5 *g.*) *salt*

In a large skillet, brown the cloves of garlic and onion until soft. Add the tomatoes, breaking them with a spoon until blended. Add the seasonings and simmer for 15 minutes. Break the tuna fish into the sauce and stir. Cook the noodles in plenty of boiling salted water. Drain. Mix the noodles and the sauce together until the noodles are covered. Serve hot, with parmesan cheese.

Macaroni and Clams

1 lb. (454 g.) shell-shaped macaroni
2 cups (450 g.) canned clams with broth
1 (28 oz. or 780 g.) can Italian plum tomatoes
1 tsp. (5 g.) sugar
½ cup (118 ml.) olive oil
¼ cup (60 ml.) white wine
3 cloves garlic, minced
2 tsp. (10 g.) freshly chopped parsley
1 tsp. (5 g.) black pepper
½ tsp. (2.5 g.) red pepper
4 sweet basil leaves

Sauté the garlic in the olive oil. Add the tomatoes and seasonings. Break the tomatoes with your spoon until mixed with the oil. Add the clams, clam broth and wine. Simmer for 5 minutes, stirring occasionally. Cook the shell macaroni in salted boiling water until *al dente*. Remove from fire and drain to a warm dish. Pour the sauce mixture over the macaroni. Serve with generous portion of parmesan cheese.

Spaghetti Vongole

1 lb. (454 g.) thin spaghetti
2 cups (450 g.) canned or frozen clams with juice
½ cup (118 ml.) olive oil
1 tsp. (5 g.) black pepper
6 cloves garlic
½ tsp. (2.5 g.) red pepper
½ cup (112 g.) fresh parsley, cut

In a saucepan, combine the olive oil, clams and clam juice (if you are using canned or fresh clams cover the clams with water, adding a chopped onion and parsley, 5 peppercorns, bring to a boil and steam until the clams open. Mince the clams and strain the broth for use). Mince the garlic and add to the broth with the seasonings. Simmer for 5 minutes. Cook the spaghetti in salted, boiling water until *al dente*. Drain and remove to warm flat soup bowls. Pour the sauce over the top, ensuring that each portion has an equal number of clams.

Clams and Linguine (*overleaf*)
A family fish favorite.

Spaghetti with Squid and Fennel

1 *lb.* (454 *g.*) *thin spaghetti*
1 *lb.* (454 *g.*) *squid*
1 *lb.* (454 *g.*) *spinach leaves*
½ *cup* (120 *ml.*) *white wine*
¼ *cup* (58 *ml.*) *olive oil*
1 *lb.* (454 *g.*) *fresh fennel*
2 *tsp.* (10 *g.*) *black pepper*
1 *onion, minced*
¼ *cup* (55 *g.*) *parsley, chopped*

Clean the squid according to the following recipe. Cut the body into rings. In a skillet, brown the onion until translucent, parboil the fennel, drain and cut into small slices. Add the fennel, spinach, wine and seasonings to the olive oil and cook for 10 minutes. Add the squid and cook for another 5 minutes. Cook the spaghetti in boiling salted water. Drain into a serving dish. Pour the sauce over the spaghetti and serve with parmesan cheese.

Squid and Ziti

Our landlady in Alvor, Portugal, created this magnificent squid stew in minutes over a charcoal fire in the garden.

1 *lb.* (454 *g.*) *ziti*
1 *lb.* (454 *g.*) *squid*
3 *cloves garlic, sliced*
2 *onions, peeled and diced*
3 *tbsp.* (42 *g.*) *freshly cut parsley*
pinch red pepper
juice of 1 lemon
¼ *cup* (58 *ml.*) *olive oil*
4 *large ripe tomatoes*
1 *tsp.* (5 *g.*) *oregano*
4 *tbsp.* (55 *g.*) *parmesan cheese*
½ *cup* (55 *g.*) *cooked peas*
½ *cup* (120 *ml.*) *red wine*

Blanch the tomatoes, peel and quarter. Sauté the garlic cloves and onion in the oil; add the tomatoes, seasonings, wine, lemon juice and cheese. Cook for 5 minutes until the tomatoes are soft. If you do not have a friendly fish store who will clean the squid for you or cannot buy it frozen, the art of cleaning squid is a simple one. Pull the tentacles and head from the tubular body. Cut the tentacles away from the eyes and slip off the outer skin. Pull the transparent spine from the sack along with the insides of the fish. Gently remove the outer purple skin under warm, running water. With large squid it is a short operation. When working with the index-finger-sized baby squid it takes a bit longer. Rinse them carefully. They should be white. Cut the squid into small pieces; if the tentacles are quite long, cut them in half. Squid reduces in size by one-third when cooked. Add the squid to the tomato mixture and cook for 10 minutes. Most people who eat squid in restaurants for the first time compare it to eating rubber. This should not be the case. Squid cooks in minutes but will become hard and chewy if boiled for several hours. Add the peas, stir quickly over a high flame. Cook the ziti in salted boiling water until *al dente*. Drain to a large bowl and stir in the sauce. Cover the pasta completely and serve with a generous helping of parmesan cheese.

Baby Squid over Spaghetti
A taste treat fresh from the Mediterranean.

Linguine with Tuna Fish and Anchovies

This is an Italian family recipe from Teresa Murchison of Buchanan Dam, Texas.

1 *lb.* (454 *g.*) *fine spaghetti*
6 *cloves garlic, minced*
1 *tsp.* (5 *g.*) *black pepper*
½ *cup* (118 *ml.*) *olive oil*
2 *cans anchovies* (10 *to* 15 *fillets*)
1 *large can tuna, drained* (½ *lb. or* 225 *g.*)

Sauté the garlic in the olive oil until brown. Cook the spaghetti in salted boiling water until *al dente*. Arrange on a hot platter, cover with the olive oil, pepper and garlic. Toss until the spaghetti is coated. Arrange the tuna fish on one side of the platter and anchovies on the other side. Serve with parmesan cheese.

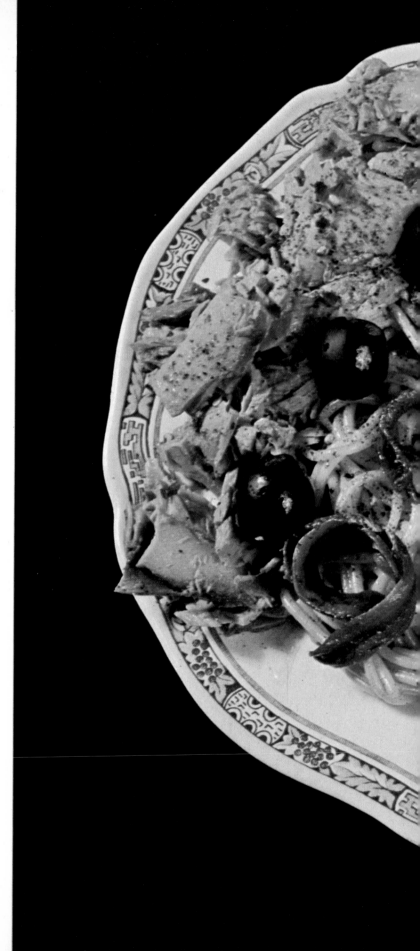

Linguine with Tuna and Anchovies
A tasty snack meal for the unexpected crowd. Wonderful with wine or beer.

Spaghetti and Crab

1 *lb.* (454 *g.*) *spaghetti*
1 *lb.* (454 *g.*) *uncooked crab meat* (3 *cans*)
2 *onions, chopped*
2 *cloves garlic, minced*
1 *tsp.* (14 *g.*) *parsley, chopped*
¼ *cup* (58 *ml.*) *olive oil*
¼ *cup* (58 *ml.*) *sherry*
4 *large ripe tomatoes*
1 *cup* (237 *ml.*) *tomato sauce*
1½ *cups* (355 *ml.*) *water*
1 *tsp.* (5 *g.*) *salt*
1 *tsp.* (5 *g.*) *sugar*
1 *tsp.* (5 *g.*) *black pepper*
½ *tsp.* (2.5 *g.*) *paprika*

Brown the onions and garlic till golden in the olive oil. Add the tomatoes (peeled), tomato sauce, water and seasonings. Simmer for 45 minutes. Add the crab and sherry. Simmer for 5 minutes more. Cook the spaghetti in rapidly boiling salted water and drain. Put on a warm serving platter and pour the crab mixture over the top. Sprinkle generously with parmesan cheese and serve.

Creamed Scallops with Noodles

36 *scallops, cut in half*
2 *cups* (475 *ml.*) *béchamel sauce* (*p.* 33)
1 *egg yolk, beaten*
½ *cup* (118 *ml.*) *dry white wine*
½ *cup* (112 *g.*) *fresh parsley*
1 *lb.* (454 *g.*) *noodles*
½ *cup* (112 *g.*) *butter*
1 *onion, minced*
paprika
¼ *cup* (112 *g.*) *butter, melted*

In a large heavy saucepan, sauté the onion in the butter. Add the halved scallops and cook for 3 minutes over a high flame. Add the wine and béchamel sauce and beaten egg yolk. Lower the heat and simmer for 5 minutes. Cook the noodles until *al dente*. Drain. Put on warm serving dishes, and mix with butter. Spoon the scallop sauce over the top of the noodles. Garnish with fresh parsley and paprika and serve immediately.

Linguine and Lobster Tails Diable

8 *lobster tails*
1 *onion, minced*
1 *tsp.* (5 *g.*) *black pepper*
½ *cup* (118 *ml.*) *olive oil*
3 *cloves garlic*
1 *lb.* (454 *g.*) *linguine*
¼ *cup* (55 *g.*) *parmesan cheese*
1 *tsp.* (5 *g.*) *red pepper*
4 *tomatoes*
¼ *cup* (55 *g.*) *parmesan cheese*
½ *cup* (118 *ml.*) *white wine*
½ *tsp.* (2.5 *g.*) *salt*
4 *basil leaves*
1 *tsp.* (5 *g.*) *chopped parsley*

Drop the lobster tails into boiling salted water. Cool and split down the middle; remove the meat. Blanch and peel two tomatoes. Brown the garlic, parsley and onion in the olive oil. Add the tomatoes, basil, seasonings and white wine. Cook for 5 minutes. Add the chopped lobster meat and simmer for a further 5 minutes. Cook the linguine until *al dente* in plenty of rapidly boiling salted water. Drain. Return to the pot and add a bit of the sauce. Toss the linguine until well-covered. Serve the linguine on separate warm plates; spoon the sauce and lobster over the top of the pasta and serve with parmesan cheese.

Fried Shrimp and Spaghetti al Burro

25 *large fresh shrimps*
$\frac{1}{4}$ *cup* (58 *ml.*) *olive oil*
$\frac{1}{4}$ *cup* (55 *g.*) *butter*
$\frac{1}{2}$ *tsp.* (2.5 *g.*) *crushed red pepper*
1 *tsp.* (5 *g.*) *freshly ground black pepper*
1 *tbsp.* (15 *ml.*) *cognac*
2 *large garlic cloves, minced*
2 *tbsp.* (28 *g.*) *minced parsley*
1 *cup* (225 *g.*) *toasted breadcrumbs*
1 *lb.* (454 *g.*) *spaghetti*
$\frac{1}{2}$ *cup* (112 *g.*) *butter*
$\frac{1}{2}$ *cup* (112 *g.*) *parmesan cheese*

Clean, remove shells and de-vein the shrimps. In a large skillet, brown the garlic, minced parsley and breadcrumbs in the olive oil and butter mixture. Add the shrimps, red pepper, salt and black pepper. Sauté over a high flame, stirring quickly and making sure the shrimps are coated with the mixture. Add 1 tbsp. (15 ml.) cognac and light with a match. Turn the skillet until all the shrimps are covered with the flaming cognac. Remove from the fire. Cook the spaghetti until *al dente* in plenty of salted boiling water and drain. Add the butter and toss until spaghetti is covered. Put on warm plates and cover with the sauce, arranging the shrimps in a pleasing pattern over the top. Generously sprinkle parmesan cheese over the pasta and serve.

Sautéed Scampi and Fettuccine Alfredo

1 *lb.* (454 *g.*) *scampi*
$\frac{1}{4}$ *cup* (58 *ml.*) *olive oil*
$\frac{1}{4}$ *cup* (55 *g.*) *butter*
2 *eggs, beaten*
1 *tbsp.* (14 *g.*) *flour*
1 *tsp.* (5 *g.*) *salt*
2 *tbsp.* (15 *ml.*) *Worcestershire sauce*
pinch red pepper
2 *tbsp.* (28 *g.*) *fresh parsley*
2 *cloves garlic*
1 *lemon rind, grated*
1 *tsp.* (5 *g.*) *oregano*
3 *tbsp.* (45 *ml.*) *lemon juice*
1 *lb.* (454 *g.*) *homemade noodles*
$\frac{1}{2}$ *cup* (112 *g.*) *butter*
2 *eggs*
2 *tsp.* (10 *g.*) *black pepper*

Clean the scampi and remove from their shells. In a bowl, mix the eggs, flour and salt. In a skillet, melt the butter in the olive oil; add the garlic and brown. Remove. Dip the shrimp into the batter and drop into the skillet. Cook till they are brown and crisp and remove. Return the garlic to the pan and add the parsley, lemon rind, lemon juice, red pepper, oregano and Worcestershire sauce. Blend quickly over a hot flame. Add the scampi but do not stir. Cook the noodles in plenty of salted boiling water until they float to the top; drain and return to the pot. Mix the eggs, pepper and butter quickly with the pasta until the noodles are coated. Put on a warm serving dish. Arrange the sautéed scampi on top of the pasta. Spoon the sauce over the whole platter and serve with additional parmesan cheese.

Summer Spaghetti

1 lb. (454 g.) spaghetti
½ cup (118 ml.) olive oil
2 cloves garlic
4 ripe tomatoes
1 (7 oz. or 196 g.) can tuna fish
pinch red pepper
½ cup (112 g.) chopped black olives
4 leaves sweet basil
2 tbsp. (28 g.) chopped parsley
2 tsp. (10 g.) black pepper
½ tsp. (2.5 g.) salt

Blanch and peel tomatoes. In a saucepan, sauté the garlic until brown and remove. Cut the tomatoes up into small pieces and add to the olive oil. Cook for 5 minutes. Add the seasonings including the garlic and stir. Cook the spaghetti until *al dente*. Drain and return to the pot. Pour the olive oil mixture over the top of the spaghetti. Toss until the spaghetti is well covered. Arrange on a platter and break up the tuna fish (drained) over the top. Garnish with the olives. Serve at room temperature, not hot.

Fisherman's Spaghetti

1 can anchovies
1 can sardines
½ cup (120 ml.) minced clams with broth
½ cup (112 g.) chopped mussels
1 cup (225 g.) cooked white fish, flaked
½ cup (118 ml.) olive oil
2 cloves garlic, minced
1 tsp. (5 g.) oregano
1 tsp. (5 g.) parsley
1 tsp. (5 g.) lemon peel, grated
2 tbsp. (30 ml.) tomato sauce
pinch red pepper
1 lb. (454 g.) short, thick macaroni

Separate the sardines, removing the bones, and mash. Brown the minced garlic in the olive oil. Add the tomato sauce and seasonings. Stir until well blended. Add the clams, broth, mussels and flaked white fish. Blend gently. Cook the macaroni until *al dente*; drain. Mix the macaroni with the fish sauce and serve with parmesan cheese.

Summer Spaghetti (*right*)
A perfect summertime luncheon.
Macaroni and Mussels (*overleaf*)
Mussels subtly flavored with onions and wine.

Spaghetti and Shrimp

1 lb. (454 g.) uncooked, peeled shrimps
4 plump, ripe tomatoes or 1 (16 oz. or 450 g.) can tomatoes
¼ cup (58 ml.) olive oil
1 onion, minced
1 crushed bay leaf
1 tsp. (5 g.) black pepper
1 lb. (454 g.) spaghetti
½ cup (120 ml.) white wine
2 tbsp. (30 ml.) tomato sauce
1 tsp. (5 g.) oregano
2 tbsp. (28 g.) chopped parsley
½ tsp. (2.5 g.) crushed red pepper
½ tsp. (2.5 g.) salt
1 tbsp. (15 ml.) lemon juice

Blanch and peel tomatoes. Sauté the onion and garlic in the olive oil. Add the tomatoes (chopped), seasonings and wine. Let the sauce simmer for 5 minutes until well-blended. Add the shrimps and cook for 5 minutes; do not overcook the shrimps. Cook the spaghetti in salted boiling water till *al dente*. Drain to a warm serving dish. Arrange the sauce over the spaghetti and serve hot with parmesan cheese.

Spaghetti with Shrimp and Peas
A quick meal for a busy Friday.

Baby Squid and Pastina

1 *lb.* (454 *g.*) *small squid* (2 *to* 3 *inches or* 5 *to* 7 *cm. long*)
2 *lb.* (900 *g.*) *ripe tomatoes*
4 *sweet basil leaves*
2 *tsp.* (10 *g.*) *black pepper*
1 *egg*
½ *cup* (112 *g.*) *fresh breadcrumbs*
¼ *cup* (55 *g.*) *parmesan cheese*
3 *cloves garlic*
1 *onion, diced*
6 *sprigs fresh parsley*
pinch red pepper
½ *cup* (118 *ml.*) *white wine*
2 *cups* (450 *g.*) *pastina*
¼ *cup* (58 *ml.*) *olive oil*

Clean the squid according to the Squid and Ziti recipe. Be careful not to break the sacks. In a large deep skillet, brown the onion and garlic until soft. Blanch and peel the tomatoes. Cut into thin slices and add to the skillet with the sweet basil, black pepper, red pepper and white wine. Simmer for 20 minutes. Mix the breadcrumbs, parmesan cheese, egg and parsley in a small bowl. With a demitasse spoon or your finger, fill the squid with ½ teaspoon (2.5 grams) of the stuffing. Do not over-fill because the stuffing swells and the squid shrinks. Drop the squid into the tomato mixture (including the tentacles) and continue to simmer. Add the pastina and cook until the pastina has absorbed the juice of the tomato. Serve hot, with additional parmesan cheese.

Squid and Lasagnette
Squid, stuffed and cooked in a tomato sauce, is equally successful over any pasta.

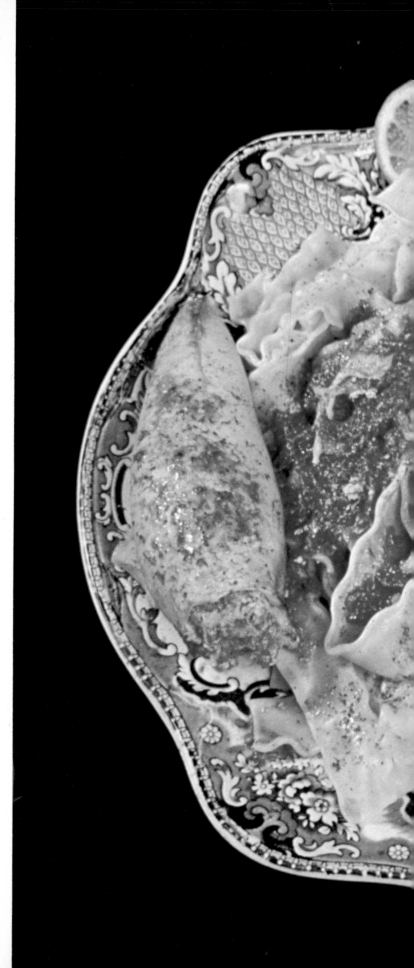

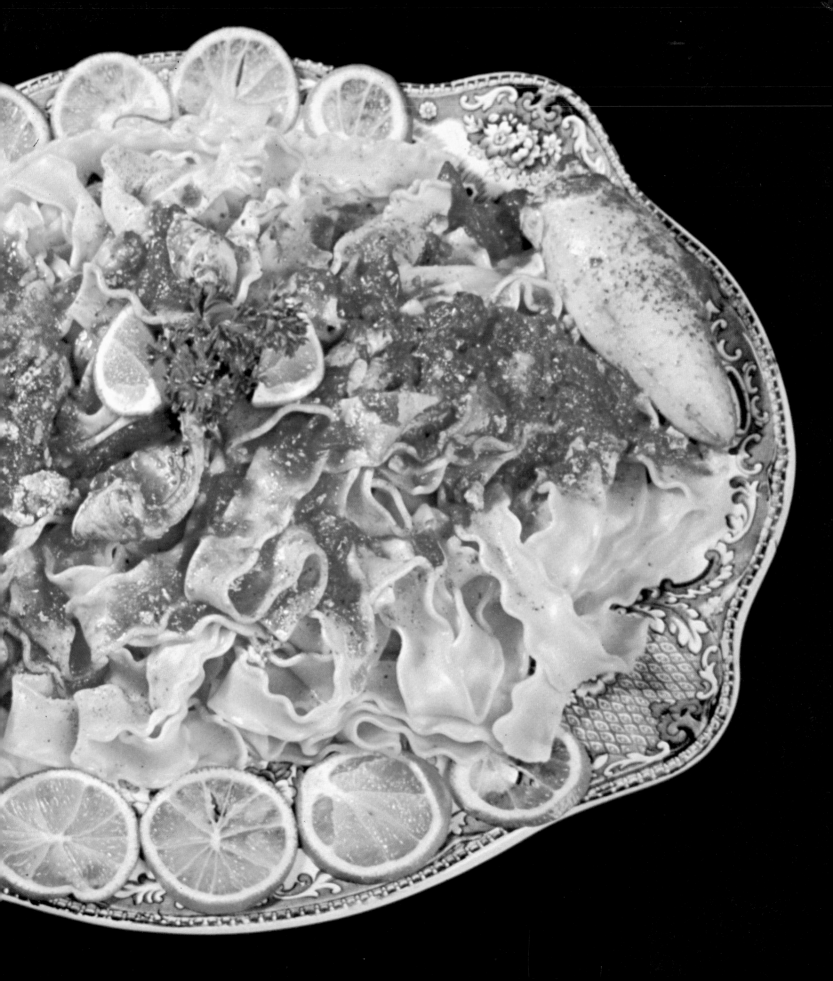

Aunt Teresa's Christmas Eve Spaghetti

1 *lb.* (454 *g.*) *baccala* (*dried cod*)
½ *cup* (118 *ml.*) *olive oil*
12 *oz.* (336 *g.*) *tomato paste*
water
1 *lb.* (454 *g.*) *spaghetti*
pinch red pepper
1 *tsp.* (5 *g.*) *oregano*
2 *tsp.* (10 *g.*) *parsley*
3 *cloves garlic, minced*
1 *tsp.* (5 *g.*) *salt*
1 *tsp.* (5 *g.*) *black pepper*

Soak the cod for 24 hours, changing the water once. Dry, remove bones and cut into small chunks. In a large skillet, sauté the garlic until brown. Add the tomato paste, stirring until mixed with the oil. Add 12 oz. (336 g.) water. Stir. Add the seasonings and cod and cook for 45 minutes. Cook the spaghetti in well-salted water until *al dente*. Remove to warm dishes and pour the cod over the top. Serve with a generous helping of parmesan cheese.

Macaroni and Mussels

1½ *quarts* (1420 *ml.*) *mussels*
½ *cup* (118 *ml.*) *white wine*
1 *onion, chopped*
2 *tbsp.* (28 *g.*) *minced parsley*
1 *lb.* (454 *g.*) *short-cut macaroni*
3 *cloves garlic, minced*
1 *tomato*
½ *cup* (118 *ml.*) *olive oil*
1 *tsp.* (5 *g.*) *grated lemon peel*

Blanch and skin the tomato. In a large skillet, brown the garlic and onion in the olive oil. Chop the tomato and add to the olive oil mixture. Stir until tomato is soft then add the white wine and seasonings. Clean the mussels, removing any hair and discarding the shells. Add the mussels to the broth and steam over a high flame, covered, for 5 minutes. Shellfish does not take long to cook. Cook the macaroni in boiling salted water until *al dente*. Drain to the skillet and mix with the mussels until the pasta is well covered. Serve hot.

Snails and Pasta Shells

Where we live in Spain we can pick quarts of snails from the vineyards after a good rain. Away from such a natural breeding ground I use canned, imported snails—do not use the frozen snails that are already stuffed with butter and seasonings, however. You do not need the shells, just the meat. If you use fresh snails, clean them by putting them into a large pot, cover with flour to cleanse the snails and cover tightly. Snails are prone to wandering. I usually keep them overnight. The next morning, cook them in rapidly boiling water, salted, for 5 minutes; rinse well (flour sticks) and remove the snail with a snail fork or toothpick.

1 *quart* (950 *ml.*) *snails, cooked*
1 *lb.* (454 *g.*) *shell macaroni*
¼ *lb.* (114 *g.*) *unsmoked bacon*
¼ *lb.* (114 *g.*) *pork, cut into cubes*
2 *onions, minced*
3 *cloves garlic*
1 *tsp.* (5 *g.*) *black pepper*
pinch hot pepper
½ *tsp.* (2.5 *g.*) *salt*
2 *tsp.* (10 *g.*) *chopped parsley*
1 *tsp.* (5 *g.*) *thyme*
1 *medium pepper* (*green*) *chopped*
4 *large plump tomatoes or* 1 (16 *oz.* or 450 *g.*) *can of tomatoes*
¼ *cup* (58 *ml.*) *olive oil*
½ *cup* (120 *ml.*) *red wine*
3 *tbsp.* (42 *g.*) *parmesan cheese*

Blanch and peel the tomatoes. Cut the bacon and pork into cubes. In a skillet, brown the garlic and onions till golden. Add the bacon and pork, cooking till done—about 10 minutes. Add the tomatoes, pepper and seasonings. Stir till the tomatoes begin to soften then add the wine. Cook the mixture for 5 minutes. Check seasonings. Add the snails and cook a further 5 minutes. Cook the shell macaroni until *al dente*. Drain and return to the pot. Add the cheese and some sauce. Mix well. Serve onto warm plates and cover the shells with the remainder of the sauce. Serve with parmesan cheese.

Baccala with Cauliflower and Spinach Noodles

2 lb. (900 g.) baccala (dried cod)
½ cup (118 ml.) olive oil
2 tsp. (10 g.) pepper
1 tsp. (5 g.) red pepper
1 lb. (454 g.) spinach noodles
¼ cup (58 ml.) olive oil
½ lb. (227 g.) unsmoked bacon, diced
6 cloves garlic
6 tbsp. (85 g.) chopped parsley
½ cup (120 ml.) white wine
1 cauliflower
freshly ground pepper

Soak the cod in cold water for 24 hours. Change the water after 12 hours. Drain, remove any bones or skin and cut the cod into cubes. Cook the cauliflower in salted water until tender then break the cauliflower into small florets. Sauté the garlic in the olive oil; add the bacon and cook until crisp. Add the cod, cooking until brown. Add the seasonings and white wine and cook for 30 minutes. Cook the green noodles until *al dente* in salted boiling water. Drain onto a heated platter and pour ¼ cup (58 ml.) olive oil over it, toss till the noodles are coated. Spread the cooked cauliflower over the top of the noodles, grind the black pepper liberally. Pour the cod over the cauliflower and serve with a garlic mayonnaise.

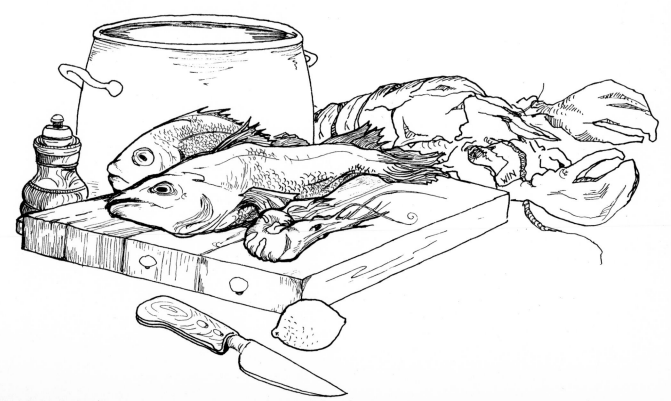

MEAT

Ziti Ballena Blanca

1 lb. (454 g.) ziti
8 slices Italian salami
4 small Italian sausages
½ cup (118 ml.) water
¼ cup (58 ml.) olive oil
3 garlic cloves
1 (28 oz. or 780 g.) can Italian tomatoes
½ tsp. (2.5 g.) salt
½ tsp. (2.5 g.) red pepper
pinch oregano
4 basil leaves
4 eggs
chopped parsley
parmesan cheese

In a heavy skillet, sauté the garlic cloves until mushy. Add the tomatoes, breaking them with a wooden spoon. Add the seasonings and salami. In a small saucepan bring the water to a boil and drop in the sausages and cook for 5 minutes. This will eliminate most of the fat content of the sausage. Drain. Drop the sausages into the skillet and continue to cook for a further 15 minutes. Cook the ziti in salted boiling water until *al dente*. Drain and return to the pot. Pour 1 tbsp. (15 ml.) of olive oil over the macaroni to keep it separate until serving. Make 4 wells in the sauce. Crack open and drop one egg into each well. Cover the skillet for about 5 minutes. Do not over-cook the eggs—they should be soft. Arrange the pasta in individual heated dishes. Put one egg in the middle of the pasta and arrange two slices of salami and one sausage on the side. Spoon the sauce over the top and garnish with parsley and a liberal sprinkling of parmesan cheese. Serve hot.

Ballena Blanca (*above*)

Macaroni Ballena Blanca (*right*)
A hearty farmhouse Saturday night supper.

Quick Meat and Spaghetti

1 lb. (454 g.) spaghetti
2 tbsp. (30 ml.) olive oil
2 cloves garlic
½ cup (112 g.) chopped onion
pinch crushed red pepper
salt and pepper
1 lb. (454 g.) ground beef
2 (6 oz. or 170 g.) cans tomato sauce
1 (6 oz. or 170 g.) can tomato paste
4 basil leaves
pinch oregano
2 tsp. (10 g.) chopped parsley

Heat the olive oil in a large skillet; add the garlic and onion, gently sautéing until the onions are golden. Add the ground beef, tomato sauce, tomato paste and seasonings. Stir well. Simmer over a low heat for 30 minutes; check your seasonings. Cook the spaghetti in a large amount of boiling salted water until *al dente*. Drain. Put the spaghetti on a warm platter and cover with the meat mixture. Sprinkle generously with parmesan cheese and serve.

Salami and Macaroni

½ lb. (227 g.) sliced Italian salami (Casa Linga)
¼ cup (58 ml.) olive oil
2 cloves garlic
½ cup (112 g.) chopped black olives
pinch oregano
½ cup (112 g.) ricotta
¼ cup (55 g.) minced parsley
½ tsp. (2.5 g.) salt
1 tsp. (5 g.) black pepper
10 anchovy fillets
1 lb. (454 g.) short-cut macaroni
¼ cup (55 g.) parmesan cheese

Cut the salami slices into small rectangular shapes. In a skillet, sauté the garlic in the olive oil until brown; add the salami, anchovies, parsley, oregano, salt and pepper. Cook gently for 5 minutes. Add the olives. Cook the short-cut macaroni in boiling salted water until *al dente*. Drain and pour into the skillet. Toss the spaghetti with the salami mixture. Add the cheeses and toss until coated. Serve immediately with additional parmesan cheese.

Spaghetti with Mortadella and Tomatoes

1 lb. (454 g.) thin spaghetti
½ lb. (227 g.) mortadella sausage
4 large tomatoes
¼ cup (58 ml.) olive oil
2 cloves garlic
1 onion, sliced
pinch oregano
2 tbsp. (28 g.) chopped parsley
pinch hot red pepper
salt and pepper
parmesan cheese

Slice the mortadella sausage and cut into cubes about ½ inch by ½ inch (1.25 cm. by (1.25 cm.) Peel the tomatoes. Cut into small pieces. In a large skillet heat the olive oil and sauté the onion and garlic until golden. Add the tomatoes, crushing with a wooden spoon till fine. Add the oregano, parsley, crushed red pepper, salt, pepper and mortadella sausage. Simmer for 10 minutes. Cook the thin spaghetti until *al dente* in plenty of boiling salted water and then drain. Toss the spaghetti with the meat mixture and serve. Sprinkle generously with parmesan cheese.

Spaghetti with Chicken Livers and Lambs' Kidneys Marinara

6 lambs' kidneys
½ lb. (227 g.) chicken livers
1 lb. (454 g.) spaghetti
½ cup (118 ml.) olive oil
2 cloves garlic
1 (28 oz. or 780 g.) can Italian tomatoes
½ tsp. (2.5 g.) black pepper
1¼ tsp. (7.5 g.) salt
1 tsp. (5 g.) oregano
2 tsp. (10 g.) chopped parsley
4 leaves fresh basil
pinch red pepper
1 tsp. (5 ml.) Worcestershire sauce

Remove the lambs' kidneys from their fat casing. Pull away the fine skin without breaking the kidney. Clean the chicken livers, carefully removing the greenish sac. Sauté the garlic in the olive oil. Add the chicken livers, brown and remove. Chop the tomatoes and add to the skillet with the pepper, red pepper, salt, oregano, parsley and sweet basil. Cook for 5 minutes until blended. Return the chicken livers to the sauce and simmer for 30 minutes. If the sauce thickens too much, dilute with ½ cup (120 ml.) of water. Cook the spaghetti in rapidly boiling, salted water until *al dente*. Drain and put the spaghetti on a warm serving dish. Spoon the sauce over the top, arranging the chicken livers and kidney in an attractive pattern. Serve immediately with parmesan cheese.

Spaghetti with Steak and Mushrooms

1 lb. (454 g.) spaghetti
1 lb. (454 g.) round steak
2 onions
¼ cup (58 ml.) olive oil
¼ cup (55 g.) butter
1 tsp. (5 g.) black pepper
1 tbsp. (15 ml.) soy sauce
2 (6 oz. or 170 g.) cans tomato paste
1 cup (237 ml.) water
½ lb. (227 g.) mushrooms
1 tsp. (5 g.) salt
pinch oregano

Lay the round steak on a board and hit it with a meat mallet until tender. Cut into small pieces. Slice the onions into small pieces. Wash and slice the mushrooms. Melt the butter in the olive oil in a large skillet and sauté the onions until golden. Brown the steak and add the mushrooms, tomato paste, water, soy sauce, salt, pepper and oregano. Simmer for 20 minutes. Cook the spaghetti in rapidly boiling, salted water until *al dente*. Drain. Combine the steak and spaghetti until the pasta is well coated. Serve on heated dishes with a generous sprinkling of parmesan cheese.

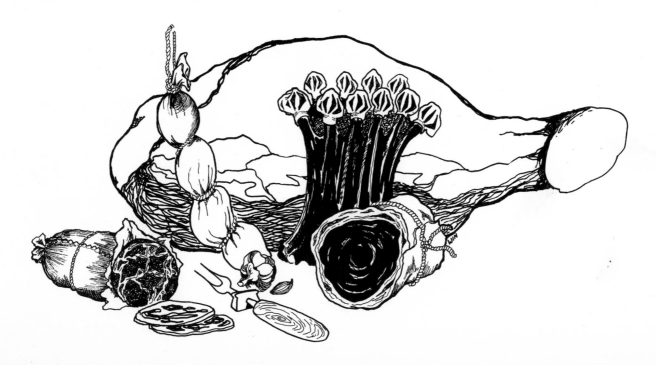

Green Noodles with Chicken Livers in Brandy

1 *lb.* (454 *g.*) *noodles*
¾ *lb.* (340 *g.*) *chicken livers*
1 *cup* (237 *ml.*) *milk*
¼ *lb.* (114 *g.*) *unsmoked bacon*
1 *onion*
2 *cloves garlic*
¼ *cup* (55 *g.*) *flour*
½ *cup* (118 *ml.*) *chicken broth*
1 *tsp.* (5 *g.*) *nutmeg*
1 *tsp.* (5 *g.*) *parsley*
½ *tsp.* (2.5 *g.*) *thyme*
¼ *cup* (58 *ml.*) *brandy*
¼ *cup* (55 *g.*) *butter*
¼ *cup* (58 *ml.*) *olive oil*
½ *cup* (112 *g.*) *sliced mushrooms*

Clean the chicken livers carefully, removing the little green sac. Put the chicken livers in a bowl, cover with milk. Chop the bacon into small pieces. Slice the garlic and onions. In a large skillet melt the butter in the olive oil, add the onions, mushrooms and garlic, and sauté till golden. Remove from the skillet. Place the diced bacon into the skillet and cook until crisp. Remove and drain the bacon; drain the chicken livers and coat them with flour. Cook quickly in the skillet. Return the mushrooms, garlic, onions and bacon to the skillet. Add the seasonings. Heat the ingredients thoroughly and add the brandy. Light the brandy and turn the skillet gently so the flame will cover the contents. Add the chicken broth and simmer for 10 minutes. Remove from heat. Cook the noodles in rapidly boiling, salted water until *al dente*. Drain. Add the noodles to the skillet and toss quickly until the pasta is well-coated. Serve with parmesan cheese.

Chicken Livers in Brandy over Spinach Noodles
Nutritious livers in a succulent wine sauce will convert your family to a new taste treat.

Veal Kidneys with Noodles   Braised Brains and Spaghetti

1 strip unsmoked bacon
2 veal kidneys (sliced)
½ lb. (227 g.) mushrooms (sliced)
¼ cup (58 ml.) olive oil
¼ cup (55 g.) butter
1 tsp. (5 g.) black pepper
1 lb. (454 g.) noodles
1 tsp. (5 g.) salt
1 cup (237 ml.) white wine
1 tsp. (5 g.) nutmeg
1 tsp. (5 g.) marjoram
2 tsp. (10 g.) chopped parsley
2 cloves garlic
1 tsp. (5 g.) grated lemon peel

Clean and soak the kidneys in milk. Wash and slice the mushrooms. Drain the kidneys and slice into small portions. Cut the bacon into small pieces. Melt the butter in the olive oil and sauté the kidney slices and bacon until brown. Remove. Sauté the mushrooms until tender; add the black pepper, nutmeg, salt, marjoram and nutmeg to the skillet. Return the veal kidney and bacon to the mixture and stir gently while simmering, for 20 minutes. Chop the garlic, parsley and lemon rind into a mince. Cook the noodles in well-salted, boiling water until *al dente*. Drain and put the pasta on a well-heated serving dish and cover the pasta with the kidney sauce. Sprinkle the garlic, parsley and lemon mixture over the top and serve immediately.

1 lb. (454 g.) brains (veal or lamb)
¼ cup (58 ml.) olive oil
2 tbsp. (30 ml.) lemon juice
1 tbsp. (14 g.) minced parsley
2 eggs
½ cup (112 g.) flour
1 cup (237 g.) chicken broth
1 tsp. (5 g.) salt
½ tsp. (2.5 g.) black pepper
½ cup (112 g.) butter
1 lb. (454 g.) spaghetti

Parboil the brains and cool. Peel the outer membrane from the brains and place in a bowl with the lemon juice, olive oil and parsley. Marinate for 15 minutes. In another small pan, heat the chicken broth. Beat the eggs, seasonings and flour making a batter. Remove the brains from the marinade and dip into the batter. Pour the marinade into a skillet and melt the butter. Over a high flame, fry the brains until brown and crispy. Remove. Add the chicken broth to the skillet, blending with the juices. Cook the spaghetti in boiling salted water and drain to the pot. Pour the sauce over the spaghetti and stir until well-coated. Pour the spaghetti onto a heated platter, arranging the brains on top. Sprinkle with parsley and parmesan cheese. Serve immediately.

Slum Gullion

This is a tasty dish that my cousin, Amy Muth of Painseville, Ohio, cooked the day before payday in the early years of her marriage. It has remained a stock recipe in the family even though economy is not now the major factor in its choice on the menu.

1 *lb.* (454 *g.*) *elbow macaroni*
3 *onions*
½ *green pepper*
2 *cloves garlic*
1 *cup* (225 *g.*) *grated American cheese*
½ *lb.* (227 *g.*) *hamburger*
salt and pepper
1 (16 *oz.* or 450 *g.*) *can tomatoes*
½ *cup* (118 *ml.*) *corn oil*

Chop the onions and pepper into small pieces. Mince the garlic. In a large skillet, sauté the onions, pepper, garlic and hamburger until brown. Add the tomatoes and seasonings. Cook for 20 minutes. In a large pot, cook in rapidly boiling salted water 1 lb. (454 g.) of elbow macaroni. Cook until tender, then drain and pour the macaroni into the skillet mixing the meat with the macaroni. Stir in the cheese and simmer until the cheese begins to melt. Serve immediately.

Macaroni Catalan

1 *lb.* (454 *g.*) *short macaroni*
½ *lb.* (227 *g.*) *pork*
½ *lb.* (227 *g.*) *sausages*
½ *lb.* (227 *g.*) *lamb*
1 (28 *oz.* or 780 *g.*) *can tomatoes*
½ *cup* (112 *g.*) *grated soft cheese*
2 *garlic cloves, minced*
2 *onions*
2 *tbsp.* (28 *g.*) *fresh, chopped parsley*
½ *cup* (118 *ml.*) *olive oil*
salt and pepper

Cut the pork, sausages and lamb into small pieces. Slice the onions. In a large skillet, sauté the pork, sausages and lamb with the garlic until brown. Add the onions, salt and pepper, stirring until the onions just begin to glaze. Stir in the tomatoes and cook gently for half-an-hour. Meanwhile, cook the macaroni in plenty of boiling salted water and drain. Add the macaroni to the skillet. Sprinkle with cheese and serve on warm plates immediately.

Spaghetti Carbonara

A truly elegant, rich pasta dish that has its origin in Northern Italy. Many restaurants and recipes call for cream but this is not authentic or necessary for a moist carbonara. It is a simple dish, prepared in a short time. The following recipe was given to me by my friend Adrian Gaye, the English film producer. Adrian, who is an excellent cook, has two specialities—Wiener Schnitzel and Spaghetti Carbonara. One can gauge the success of his latest project with the choice of dish he serves. When we were struggling to produce a film together several years ago, more often than not it was Spaghetti Carbonara served with Italian bread, tomato salad and wine. Economic but a dish of gourmet standard.

1 *lb.* (454 *g.*) *spaghetti*
1 *lb.* (454 *g.*) *thick unsmoked bacon*
¾ *lb.* (340 *g.*) *fresh mushrooms*
6 *cloves garlic*
5 *eggs*
¼ *cup* (55 *g.*) *black pepper*
2 *onions, sliced*
¼ *cup* (58 *ml.*) *olive oil*
½ *lb.* (227 *g.*) *freshly grated parmesan*

Bring an 8 quart (7½ liter) kettle to the boil. Cut the bacon into small chunks. Slice and chop the onion. Wash and slice the mushrooms. Mince the cloves of garlic. In a heavy skillet, heat the olive oil and add the bacon, cooking until crisp. Remove. Sauté the onions, mushrooms and garlic until golden brown. Return the bacon to the mixture and keep warm. Cook the spaghetti in the now boiling salted water until *al dente*. Meanwhile, beat 5 eggs and pepper in a bowl. Add the cheese, stirring well. Stir in the mushroom-bacon mixture. Drain the spaghetti and immediately pour into the bowl, tossing the pasta rapidly with the egg mixture until coated. The heat of the spaghetti will cook the eggs. Serve immediately.

Spaghetti Carbonara (*overleaf*)
A simple dish, enhanced by bacon and eggs, that is becoming increasingly popular as a luncheon dish.

TRENCHERMAN'S FARE

Many of the following recipes are suitable for special occasions—Sunday lunch, main dishes for a buffet supper or party dinners. The essence is in the slow cooking, be it top of the stove in a heavy kettle, or simmering in a warm oven until the juices and ingredients have blended.

Main Dish Meals

Stuffed Manicotti

Why not double the recipe and freeze one pan until you need it?

1 *lb.* (454 *g.*) *sweet Italian sausage cut into pieces*
1 *lb.* (454 *g.*) *ground beef*
1 *onion, minced*
¼ *cup* (58 *ml.*) *olive oil*
2 (16 *oz. or 475 ml.*) *cans tomato puree*
1 (6 *oz. or 170 g.*) *can tomato paste*
1 *tsp.* (5 *g.*) *sweet basil*
2 *pinches of sugar*
1 *cup* (225 *g.*) *butter*
1¾ *tsp.* (8 *g.*) *salt*
½ *tsp.* (2.5 *g.*) *pepper*
1 (8 *oz. or 225 g.*) *package Manicotti*
2 *lb.* (900 *g.*) *ricotta*
½ *lb.* (227 *g.*) *mozzarella, diced*
2 *tsp.* (10 *g.*) *chopped parsley*
parmesan cheese
1 *tsp.* (5 *g.*) *freshly ground pepper*

In a deep skillet or Dutch oven, brown the sausage in the olive oil. Remove to absorbent paper. Spoon off the fat from the pan. Brown the beef and onion. Stir in the tomato purée and paste. Blend with a spoon. Add the basil, salt, sugar, pepper and water. Bring to a boil and simmer, covered, for 45 minutes. Add the sausage and cook for another 15 minutes. Meanwhile, begin to boil the Manicotti shells in plenty of salted water. Combine the cheeses, chopped parsley, one pinch of sugar, 1 tsp. (5 g.) freshly ground pepper in a bowl. When the Manicotti are done (*al dente*) drain and place on a wet cloth. Stuff the cheeses into the shells. Spoon some of the tomato sauce into a rectangular baking dish approximately 13 by 9 inches (33 by 23 cm.). Arrange the stuffed Manicotti evenly in the dish. Pour the remaining sauce over the top. Sprinkle with parmesan cheese. Bake 30 minutes in a pre-heated hot (375°) oven and serve.

Stuffed Manicotti
Cheese stuffed tubes of pasta that challenge lasagne as a party favorite.

Farfalle Almond Casserole

1 *package* (¾ *lb. or* 350 *g.) farfalle (butterflies) macaroni*
2 *tbsp.* (28 *g.) butter*
½ *lb.* (227 *g.) mushrooms*
4 *tbsp.* (55 *g.) butter*
½ *cup* (112 *g.) slivered almonds*
½ *cup* (112 *g.) minced onion*
½ *tsp.* (2.5 *g.) salt*
1½ *cups* (355 *ml.) chicken broth*
3 *tbsp.* (42 *g.) flour*
2 *tbsp.* (28 *g.) chopped parsley*

Put the water on to boil for the noodles. Cook the mushrooms, onion and salt, until golden. Cook the noodles for 5 minutes in the rapidly boiling, salted water. Drain. Put the noodles into the mushroom-onion mixture in the skillet. Turn the noodle mixture into a bowl and pour the chicken broth over the top of the noodles, using a fork to ensure an even distribution of the broth. Melt the butter in a small saucepan. Add the almonds and gently shake the pan. Add the flour gradually, stirring constantly as it thickens. Add the almonds to the noodle mixture, stirring gently. Pour into a well-greased casserole and bake for 30 minutes in a moderately hot (375°) oven. Garnish with parsley and chopped almonds.

Macaroni and Cheese

Topping:
2 *tbsp.* (28 *g.) butter*
8 *oz.* (225 *g.) elbow macaroni*
½ *lb.* (225 *g.) grated sharp cheese*
2 *cups* (450 *g.) breadcrumbs*
¼ *cup* (55 *g.) butter*

Sauce:
1 *tbsp.* (14 *g.) butter*
½ *tsp.* (2.5 *g.) salt*
½ *tsp.* (2.5 *g.) nutmeg*
1 *cup* (237 *ml.) milk*
1 *tbsp.* (14 *g.) flour*
1 *tbsp.* (14 *g.) minced onion*
½ *tsp.* (2.5 *g.) black pepper*

Cook the elbow macaroni until *al dente*. Drain. Return to the pot with ¼ cup (55 g.) butter and mix well. While the macaroni is cooking, make the sauce thus: in a saucepan melt the butter. Add the flour, stirring continually until blended. Gradually add the milk, stirring to ensure its smoothness. Add the onion, nutmeg, salt and pepper and almost all the grated cheese—reserve some cheese to put on

the top. Simmer until the cheese has melted. Add the sauce to the macaroni, stirring until the macaroni is well covered. Pour into a well-greased casserole. Melt 2 tbsp. (28 g.) butter in a skillet and add the soft breadcrumbs. Gently shake the skillet until the breadcrumbs have absorbed the butter. Pour over the casserole and sprinkle the remaining cheese on top. Bake in a moderate (350°) oven for 30 minutes.

Simple Macaroni and Cheese

½ *lb.* (227 *g.) elbow macaroni*
1½ *cups* (337 *g.) shredded sharp cheese*
¾ *tsp.* (4 *g.) salt*
2 *cups* (475 *ml.) milk*
3 *tomatoes*
4 *tbsp.* (55 *g.) butter*
black pepper

Cook the elbow macaroni until *al dente*. Drain and place a layer of the macaroni in a greased casserole and sprinkle with cheese, salt and pepper. Dot with butter. Continue layering the macaroni with the cheese and seasonings until you reach the top. Pour the milk over the whole mixture. Slice the tomatoes and arrange on top. Dot with the remaining butter and bake in a moderate (350°) oven for 40 minutes.

Baked Fettuccine

1 *package* (¾ *lb. or* 350 *g.) green egg noodles*
6 *tbsp.* (85 *g.) butter*
1 *cup* (237 *ml.) sour cream*
2 *tbsp.* (28 *g.) minced onion*
4 *oz.* (112 *g.) parmesan cheese*
1 *cup* (237 *ml.) evaporated milk*
1 *tsp.* (5 *g.) salt*
½ *tsp.* (2.5 *g.) pepper*
½ *tsp.* (2.5 *g.) nutmeg*

Cook the noodles in salted, boiling water until *al dente*. Meanwhile, in a skillet melt the butter and sauté the onions until golden. Drain the noodles into the skillet and stir. Pour the sour cream over the noodles, coating them, and simmer over a low flame. Add the milk, salt, pepper and 3 tbsp. (42 g.) parmesan cheese. Pour the mixture into a greased casserole. Sprinkle 1 oz. (28 g.) of cheese over the top and bake for 15 minutes.

Summer Camp Macaroni

I remember that to ensure the quick feeding of our horde, a large covered metal roaster, insulated by newspaper and a table cloth was carried with us from the city and was duly unwrapped by my mother, the first night we arrived at summer camp in the Adirondacks. Our family sat around the round dining-room table—the tiffany shaded kerosene lamp overhead shadowing the hungry stares as our eyes focused on the emerging food. Childhood experiences are often exaggerated, I know, in our memories but I can still recall the scent of the aromatic mist rising from that blue pan as the cover was lifted, stimulating the salivary glands into a Pavlovian response. Nirvana! Here is the recipe.

2 pints (946 ml.) Italian meatball sauce (p. 33)
1 lb. (454 g.) ricotta
½ lb. (227 g.) parmesan cheese
½ cup (112 g.) freshly chopped parsley
3 eggs, beaten
¼ cup (55 g.) black pepper
1½ lb. (680 g.) rigatoni or ziti

Boil the rigatoni in a large kettle with plenty of salted water. While you are waiting, mix the ricotta, parsley, eggs and black pepper until smooth. Drain the ricotta. In a large roasting pan, spoon some of the tomato sauce. Break up the meatballs into quarters. Arrange a layer of the pasta, sprinkle the cheese mixture and cover with the sauce. Sprinkle parmesan cheese over the layer; place meatballs on the top. Repeat this pattern of pasta, sauce, cheese mix, parmesan cheese and meatballs until you have filled the pan. Cover the roaster with its lid and bake in a moderate (350°) oven for 40 minutes. Do not lift the lid. Cover immediately with several layers of newspaper and a large tablecloth. The pasta will retain the heat for several hours.

Rigatoni Milanese

1 package (¾ lb. or 350 g.) rigatoni
1 pint (473 ml.) Italian tomato sauce (p. 138)
½ lb. (227 g.) ground beef
½ lb. (227 g.) ground pork
¾ cup (170 g.) toasted breadcrumbs
1 tsp. (5 g.) parsley
½ cup (112 g.) parmesan cheese
1 cup (225 g.) parmesan cheese
2 eggs, beaten
1 tsp. (5 g.) salt
¼ tsp. (1.25 g.) garlic powder
1 tsp. (5 g.) black pepper
pinch red pepper

Cook the rigatoni in salted boiling water. Meanwhile, in a bowl combine the meat, breadcrumbs, parsley, cheese, eggs, salt, garlic powder and black pepper and mix thoroughly. Drain the rigatoni onto a damp cloth. Stuff the tubes with the mixture. Spoon some of the tomato sauce onto the bottom of a buttered rectangular baking dish. Arrange the rigatoni in a layer. Cover with tomato sauce, sprinkle the layer with parmesan cheese and repeat the layers until you have used up the stuffed rigatoni. Cover with aluminum foil and bake in a moderate (350°) oven for an hour Uncover and bake a further 15 minutes, or until brown on top.

Rigatoni with Chicken (overleaf)
Tomato sauce with delicate chicken quarters is an excellent party dish. For chicken sauce recipe see page 147.

Baked Cut Ziti

This is another delicious recipe from my buttonhole Aunt Mary Brindisi of Utica, New York.

1 *lb.* (454 g.) *ziti*
1 *lb.* (454 g.) *ground beef*
½ *lb.* (227 g.) *pork, ground*
½ *lb.* (227 g.) *veal, ground*
½ *cup* (112 g.) *parmesan cheese*
1 *cup* (225 g.) *fresh breadcrumbs*
parmesan cheese
3 *eggs, beaten*
3 *tbsp.* (55 g.) *parsley*
pinch red pepper
1 *tsp.* (5 g.) *salt*
¼ *cup* (58 ml.) *olive oil*
1 *pint* (473 ml.) *tomato sauce*

In a large skillet, heat the olive oil. Sauté the garlic cloves until golden. Mix the meat, cheese (½ cup or 112 grams), breadcrumbs, eggs, parsley, red pepper and salt in a bowl. Fry the meat mixture very slowly in the olive oil. Add the tomato sauce and simmer for 1 hour. Boil the ziti in plenty of boiling, salted water and drain. Into a rectangular buttered baking dish spoon some sauce. Place a layer of ziti and cover with additional sauce. Sprinkle with parmesan cheese and continue to layer the pasta and sauce until the pan is full. Bake for 1 hour in a moderately hot (350°) oven.

Harriet's Spaghetti Soufflé

½ *lb.* (227 g.) *thin spaghetti*
2 *tbsp.* (28 g.) *butter*
2 *tbsp.* (28 g.) *flour*
1 *cup* (237 ml.) *scalded milk*
2 *tbsp.* (28 g.) *chopped onion*
2 *tbsp.* (28 g.) *chopped pepper*
1 *tbsp.* (14 g.) *of parsley*
3 *eggs, separated*
1 (8 oz. or 225 g.) *can of mushrooms*
salt and pepper
1 *cup* (237 ml.) *tomato sauce*
½ *cup* (112 g.) *parmesan cheese*

In a saucepan melt the butter, add the flour and blend. Slowly add the milk until the sauce thickens. Now add the cheese, cooking until the cheese melts and the sauce is smooth. Add the onion, pepper, parsley, mushrooms, salt and pepper. Separate the eggs. Mix the yolks with the sauce. Cook the pasta in plenty of salted boiling water and drain. Mix the pasta with the cheese sauce. Beat the egg whites until stiff and fold in the spaghetti with the cheese sauce. Bake in a greased casserole in a slow (325°) oven for 40 minutes. Serve with a plain tomato sauce.

Clams in Fried Pasta Shells

½ *lb.* (227 g.) *large shell macaroni*
¼ *cup* (58 ml.) *olive oil*
3 *garlic cloves, minced*
1 (6 oz. or 170 g.) *can minced clams*
1 (8 oz. or 225 g.) *package cream cheese*
¼ *tsp.* (1.5 g.) *tabasco sauce*
2 *tsp.* (10 g.) *minced onion*

Cook the macaroni in well-salted boiling water. Drain. In a large skillet, sauté the garlic and onions until golden. Add the shells, three or four at a time, cooking until golden. Let them cool on absorbent paper. In a bowl mix the cream cheese, drained clams and tabasco sauce. Add a bit of the clam broth to ensure a smooth creamy texture. Fill the fried shells with the cream mixture. Keep warm

Macaroni Loaf

I remember vividly during the 'ration' days of World War II, the cumulative groans that emerged from the dining hall when Macaroni Loaf was served once again! We had dutifully handed in our food ration books at the beginning of term and I am sure those sweet-faced dietitians in their starched uniforms spent hours in their laboratory kitchens conceiving new ways to serve meatless dishes. Macaroni emerged in rings with creamed Spam—loaves with stewed tomatoes and the inevitable red pimiento and green olives to add an 'exotic' touch to the meal. Such was the fare of emerging intellectuals. The lasting effect, however, is my life-long aversion to red pimientos and stuffed green olives in any sauce. A simple dish if cooked with good ingredients and well-seasoned, needs no embellishment. Here is a recipe for Macaroni Loaf that relies on its own merits for excellent flavor.

4 oz. (112 g.) short-cut macaroni
1 cup (237 ml.) milk
2 tbsp. (28 g.) butter
1 cup (225 g.) sharp cheddar
1 tsp. (5 g.) salt
½ tsp. (2.5 g.) freshly ground pepper
1 cup (225 g.) soft breadcrumbs
1 egg, beaten
1 tbsp. (14 g.) parsley
2 tbsp. (28 g.) minced onion
pinch of nutmeg
1 cup (237 ml.) marinara sauce (p. 138)

Cook the pasta in plenty of boiling, salted water. In a saucepan melt the butter and add the onion and breadcrumbs. Stir until they are brown. Add the milk and cheese. Simmer until the cheese melts. Combine the sauce with the beaten egg, parsley, salt, pepper and nutmeg. Drain the pasta and mix with the sauce in the pan. Pour into a well-greased loaf tin. Set in a pan of water (1 inch or 2.5 cm. deep) and bake for 1 hour in a moderate oven until firm. Serve with marinara sauce.

Pasta and Breast of Chicken Casserole

6 chicken breasts
¼ cup (58 ml.) olive oil
3 cups (711 ml.) chicken broth
½ cup (55 g.) sliced mushrooms
½ lb. (227 g.) Italian sausage, diced
1 cup (237 ml.) dry white wine
⅓ cup (75 g.) parmesan cheese
1½ cups (337 g.) stellitti pastina
2 tbsp. (28 g.) fresh parsley
4 scallions, chopped

Remove the bone from the breasts. In a large skillet, brown the chicken on all sides and remove. Sauté the sausages and add the scallions and mushrooms. Arrange the chicken breasts in a rectangular-shaped greased casserole and pour the chicken broth and wine over the breasts. Add the sausage, mushrooms, scallions and cheese. Sprinkle the uncooked pastina into the pan. Stir the broth so that the pastina, mushrooms and scallions are covered. Bake in a moderate (350°) oven for 40 minutes. Add more broth if the mixture becomes too dry.

Baked Ziti Katalanita

2 pints (946 ml.) of marinara sauce (page 138)
1 lb. (454 g.) ziti
2 (15 oz. or 400 g.) cartons ricotta
½ lb. (227 g.) package mozzarella, cubed
½ cup (112 g.) parmesan cheese
2 tsp. (10 g.) freshly cut parsley
2 tbsp. (28 g.) black pepper
½ tsp. (2.5 g.) salt
parmesan cheese
2 eggs

Boil the ziti in salted water until *al dente*. In a bowl, mix the cheeses, parsley, pepper and eggs. Blend until smooth. Drain the macaroni and return to the pan. In a buttered casserole place a layer of the ziti, spoon the cheese mixture evenly across the top and cover the cheese with the marinara sauce. Sprinkle with additional parmesan. Continue to arrange the layers in the same order, ending with a topping of parmesan cheese. Bake in a moderate oven for 40 minutes, uncovered.

Ziti Katalinita (*overleaf*)
A delicious rich casserole.

Macaroni Timbale

Pastry Dough:

3 *cups* (675 g.) *flour, sifted*
1 *cup* (225 g.) *sugar*
3 *egg yolks*
1½ *cups* (337 g.) *butter*
2 *tsp.* (10 g.) *grated lemon peel*

Mix the flour and butter together until the mixture is the size of small peas. Add the sugar, lemon rind and egg yolks. Blend with your fingers until a smooth pastry is formed. Cool the dough in the refrigerator for half-an-hour.

1 *lb.* (454 g.) *macaroni cut into lengths*
½ *lb.* (227 g.) *mushrooms*
4 *oz.* (112 g.) *giblets*
4 *oz.* (112 g.) *sweetbreads*
4 *tomatoes, peeled and diced*
1 *onion, minced*
1 *cup* (237 ml.) *meat sauce* (p. 139)
¼ *cup* (55 g.) *butter*
½ *tsp.* (2½ g.) *salt*
1 *tsp.* (5 g.) *black pepper, ground*
½ *tsp.* (2½ g.) *nutmeg*
½ *cup* (120 ml.) *dry white wine*
1 *cup* (237 ml.) *béchamel sauce* (p. 33)
½ *cup* (112 g.) *parmesan cheese*

Boil the short-cut macaroni in plenty of salted water. Cook until *al dente*. Meanwhile in a skillet, melt the butter and sauté the onion. Parboil the sweetbreads for 3 minutes, rinse and remove the outer skin. Cut the sweetbreads and giblets into small pieces, add the wine and cook on high flame in the skillet, until the wine evaporates. Add the mushrooms, tomatoes, salt, black pepper and nutmeg. Drain the macaroni into a large bowl and pour the meat mixture over the macaroni, stirring until it is well coated. Stir in 1 cup of meat sauce, 1 of béchamel sauce and the cheese.

Roll out three-quarters of the pastry dough to ¼ inch (64 mm.) thickness. Line a greased, deep casserole with the dough and pour in the macaroni mixture. Roll out the remainder of the dough and cover the top, sealing in the macaroni. Cut a slash in the top for escaping steam. Bake in a preheated hot (375°) oven for 30 minutes, or until the pastry is brown on top.

Macaroni, Oyster and Sweetbread Timbale

Pastry Dough:

Use the same pastry as in Macaroni Timbale

4 *oz.* (112 g.) *short-cut macaroni*
1 *pint* (473 ml.) *milk*
4 *egg yolks*
½ *cup* (118 ml.) *cream*
1 *cup* (225 g.) *sliced mushrooms*
2 *tbsp.* (28 g.) *minced onion*
1 *tomato, minced*
½ *tsp.* (2.5 g.) *salt*
1 *tsp.* (5 g.) *pepper*
½ *tsp.* (2.5 g.) *cayenne pepper*
1 *tsp.* (5 g.) *parsley flakes*
½ *lb.* (227 g.) *sweetbreads*
12 *oysters* (*fresh*)

Make your pastry dough and place in the refrigerator for an hour. Bring the milk to a simmer (do not boil) and add the macaroni lengths. Cook until the macaroni is soft, about 15 minutes. Add the salt, pepper, cayenne pepper, parsley flakes, onions, tomato and mushroom slices. Stir in the cream and egg yolks until smooth. Rinse the oysters. Blanch the sweetbreads and remove the outer membrane. Cut into small pieces. Combine the macaroni mixture with the sweetbreads and oysters. Roll the pastry to ¼ inch (64 mm.) thickness. Grease a deep casserole and line the dish with three-quarters of the pastry. Pour the macaroni mixture into the pastry shell. Cover with the remaining pastry and seal. Make holes with a fork in the top of the pastry and bake in a hot oven (375°) for half-an-hour, or until brown. Cool and serve.

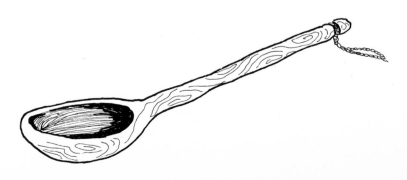

Shrimp and Macaroni Casserole

1 pkt. (12 oz. or 336 g.) wide noodles
3 tbsp. (42 g.) butter
2 tbsp. (28 g.) flour
2 cups (475 ml.) milk
1 onion, minced
2 tbsp. (30 ml.) tomato purée
½ cup (112 g.) parmesan cheese
½ tsp. (2.5 g.) tabasco sauce
1 tsp. (5 g.) salt
1 tsp. (5 g.) black pepper
½ cup (118 ml.) cream
½ cup (118 ml.) white wine
1 lb. (454 g.) fresh shrimps
2 tbsp. (28 g.) butter

Cook the wide noodles in plenty of boiling, salted water. In a saucepan, melt the butter and sauté the onion until golden. Add the flour, blending until smooth. Add the milk slowly, until well blended. Add the wine, tabasco sauce, salt, pepper and cream. Cook until thickened. Add the shrimp and taste for seasoning. Pour the shrimp mixture over the macaroni, mixing until the noodles are covered. Pour the mixture into a buttered casserole. Sprinkle with the parmesan cheese, dot with butter and bake in a hot oven for 30 minutes until brown on top.

Macaroni and Pork Chop Casserole (overleaf)
Layers of farfalle (butterflies), tomato sauce and pork chops combine to satisfy the most robust appetite.

Salmon and Macaroni Soufflé

½ lb. (227 g.) shell macaroni
1 lb. (454 g.) can salmon
3 tbsp. (42 g.) butter
1 tbsp. (14 g.) minced onion
2 tbsp. (28 g.) flour
½ tsp. (2.5 g.) salt
1 tsp. (5 g.) pepper
2 cups (475 ml.) milk
½ cup (118 ml.) dry white wine
1 tbsp. (14 g.) grated lemon rind
2 tbsp. (28 g.) slivered almonds
3 eggs, separated
1 tbsp. (14 g.) fresh parsley, minced

Cook the shell macaroni until *al dente* in plenty of boiling salted water. In a saucepan melt the butter. Sauté the onion until brown, add the flour, blending to a smooth paste. Slowly add the milk, stirring vigorously. Add the wine, almonds, salt, pepper and lemon rind. Separate the eggs and add the yolks to the mixture. Drain the macaroni, and pour into a saucepan. Grease a soufflé dish with butter. Beat the egg whites until stiff and fold them into the mixture. Turn into the soufflé dish and place in a large pan of water in the oven. Bake for 1 hour in a slow (300-325°) oven.

Macaroni and Pork Chop Casserole

1 lb. (454 g.) farfalle (butterfly)
1 pint (475 ml.) marinara sauce (p. 138)
6 pork chops
½ cup (112 g.) parmesan cheese
¼ cup (58 ml.) olive oil
3 cloves garlic
2 tsp. (10 g.) fresh parsley
1 tbsp. (14 g.) fresh lemon rind

In a heavy skillet, brown the pork chops in the olive oil. Remove from the pan and sauté the garlic in the oil until soft. Add the parsley and lemon rind. Cook the farfalle in a large pot with plenty of boiling salted water, drain and return to the pot. Add the garlic mixture from the skillet, the marinara sauce and cheese to the pasta. Mix well. Arrange half the pork chops in a layer in a greased casserole. Pour half the farfalle mixture over the top; make another layer of the pork chops and farfalle, sprinkle with parmesan cheese and bake in a slow oven for 40 minutes.

Macaroni and Eggplant

1 lb. (454 g.) curly macaroni
1 large eggplant (about 1 lb. or 450 g.)
1 (28 oz. or 780 g.) can tomatoes
¼ cup (58 ml.) olive oil
1 onion
2 cloves garlic
butter
1 tsp. (5 g.) thyme
1 tsp. (5 g.) salt
1 tsp. (5 g.) pepper
pinch red pepper
¼ cup (58 ml.) white wine
parmesan cheese

Cook the macaroni in plenty of boiling, salted water until al dente. In a large skillet, sauté the onion and garlic until soft. Cut the tomatoes into small pieces and add to the skillet crushing them with your spoon. Add the wine, thyme, salt, black pepper and pinch of crushed red pepper to the mixture. Cook slowly for 10 minutes. Wash and cut the eggplant into small cubes and add to the tomato mixture, cooking for another 10 minutes. Drain the macaroni. Pour half the macaroni into a buttered baking dish. Sprinkle parmesan cheese over the macaroni; spoon half the tomato-eggplant mixture over the pasta. Add the remaining pasta and cover with the eggplant sauce. Sprinkle with parmesan cheese and dot with butter. Bake in a moderate oven (350°) for 30 minutes.

Ham and Noodle Bake

1 lb. (454 g.) smoked raw ham, sliced
1 lb. (454 g.) wide noodles
1 pint (473 ml.) béchamel sauce (p. 33)
butter
1 fennel
1 can asparagus (12 stalks)
parmesan cheese

Parboil the fennel until just done, remove and cut into small strips. Cook the noodles until al dente in plenty of boiling salted water. Spoon a little béchamel sauce into a greased casserole. Arrange one-third of the noodles. Cover with part of the sliced ham. Arrange either the asparagus or fennel on top of the ham. Spoon the béchamel sauce over, to cover. Continue layering the noodles with the ham, asparagus or fennel and béchamel sauce. Sprinkle parmesan cheese and butter over the top and bake in a hot oven for 20 minutes, until brown on top.

Spaghetti with Stuffed Artichokes

4 artichokes
3 cups (711 ml.) water
2 egg yolks
½ lb. (227 g.) pork loin, minced
¼ lb. (114 g.) Italian sausage, without casing
¼ cup (58 ml.) olive oil
4 crushed garlic cloves
2 tbsp. (28 g.) crushed almonds
1 (6 oz. or 170 g.) can tomato paste
1½ cups (355 ml.) water
pinch of crushed red pepper
1 tbsp. (15 ml.) oil
1 tbsp. (14 g.) flour
½ cup (118 ml.) wine

Clean the artichokes and cut the tips of the leaves from them. Bang each one very hard on the table and cut in half and remove the hairy covering of the artichoke heart with a sharp knife. Place the artichokes in the water and boil until just tender. Remove. In a small bowl, mix the pork, sausage meat and egg yolks. Stuff the center of each artichoke half with the mixture. In a large saucepan, combine the olive oil, garlic, almonds, tomato paste, water, salt and red pepper. Cook until the sauce begins to boil. Mix the oil and flour in a small bowl and add it gradually to the sauce. Place the stuffed artichokes in the sauce, simmer for half-an-hour. Add a half-cup of wine and simmer for another 10 minutes. Serve over spaghetti al burro.

Shells Stuffed with Tuna Fish

1 lb. (454 g.) large shells
2 (6 oz. or 170 g.) cans tuna fish
6 anchovy fillets
¼ cup (55 g.) chopped parsley
1 tbsp. (15 ml.) lemon juice
1 tsp. (5 g.) pepper
½ tsp. (2.5 g.) salt
½ cup (112 g.) fresh breadcrumbs
2 eggs
1 pint (475 ml.) béchamel sauce (p. 33)
paprika
¼ cup (55 g.) parmesan cheese
butter

Cook the shells in plenty of boiling salted water. While the shells are cooking, combine the eggs, salt, pepper, chopped parsley, tuna, anchovies, lemon juice and breadcrumbs. Drain the shells and place on a wet towel. Stuff the shells with the tuna mixture and arrange in a rectangular, greased casserole. Cover with the béchamel sauce. Sprinkle with paprika and parmesan cheese. Dot with butter and bake in a moderate oven for 30 minutes until brown on top.

"Red as Fire" Macaroni

This is one of my cousin Marie Panella Jones', of San Antonio, Texas, favorite recipes. It is indeed red as fire!

¼ cup (58 ml.) olive oil
4 cloves garlic
salt
6 large dry sweet peppers
1 lb. (454 g.) large macaroni (rigatoni)

Put a pan of salted water on to boil. In an iron skillet, heat the oil and three of the garlic cloves. Fry for a couple of minutes and then add the dry peppers. As soon as these have swelled and become shiny (be careful not to burn them), remove from oil and crush them adding the fired garlic. You should obtain a sauce. Pour the pasta into the boiling water and cook al dente. When the pasta is almost ready pour a few tablespoons of oil into a pan with the fourth garlic clove and fry until golden. Add the pepper sauce, stirring it quickly into the oil so that it will not blacken. Drain the pasta and dress it with the sauce. The pasta will be 'Red as Fire'.

Macaroni Stuffed Peppers

4 large green peppers
1 cup (225 g.) cooked ditali
½ lb. (227 g.) ground beef
2 tbsp. (28 g.) minced onion
2 cloves garlic
½ tsp. (2.5 ml.) Worcestershire sauce
1 tomato, peeled and quartered
¼ cup (58 ml.) olive oil
parsley
1 tsp. (5 g.) chopped parsley
1 egg
½ cup (112 g.) parmesan cheese
1 tsp. (5 g.) salt
½ tsp. (2.5 g.) pepper
1 cup (225 g.) cooked peas
sweet basil
1 (16 oz. or 450 g.) can tomatoes
¼ cup (60 ml.) white wine

In a skillet, sauté the onion and garlic till brown. Add the ground beef and tomato. Cook till the meat has lost its red color. Combine with the macaroni, parsley, egg, cheese, salt and pepper. Cut the peppers in half, lengthwise. Strip away the white undercoating and seeds. Stuff the peppers with the above mixture and arrange in a rectangular baking dish. Cover the peppers with the tomatoes and peas. Dribble a little olive oil across the top. Place the sweet basil and parsley on top. Add the wine and bake in a moderate oven (350°) for 40 minutes, or until brown on top.

Italian Veal and Noodles

1½ lb. (680 g.) rolled shoulder of veal
¼ cup (55 g.) butter
1 quart (950 ml.) of water
2 chicken bouillon cubes
1 tsp. (5 g.) salt
1 onion, minced
1 carrot, chopped
1 tsp. (5 g.) black pepper
1 tsp. (5 g.) nutmeg
1 package noodles (¾ lb. or 350 g.)
1 parsnip (chopped)
2 cloves garlic
2 tsp. (10 g.) tomato paste
1 tsp. (5 g.) rosemary
pinch of oregano
juice of 1 lemon
½ cup (112 g.) shredded mild cheese
½ cup (118 ml.) cream
½ lb. (227 g.) mushrooms
green olives (optional)

In a large, flameproof casserole, brown the shoulder of veal on all sides. Remove. Add the water, bouillon cubes, salt, onion, carrot, black pepper, nutmeg, parsnip, garlic, tomato paste, oregano and lemon juice. Stir well. Bring to a boil and return the veal to the casserole. Cook for 1 hour until the veal is tender. Remove and cool. Meanwhile, cook the noodles in plenty of boiling salted water for 5 minutes. Slice and then cut into bite sized pieces. You should have about 2 cups (450 ml.) of stock. Spoon the fat from the top. Add the veal. Wash and slice the mushrooms. Drain the noodles which are not quite cooked and add to the veal mixture. Stir in the cheese, cream and mushrooms. Place in a pre-heated moderate (350°) oven for 45 minutes. Garnish with green olives.

Italian Veal and Noodles
A supper party is the perfect setting for this delicately flavored dish.

Substantial Sauces and Consorts

Aromatic sauces, bubbling on the stove forecast epicurean feasts. I am highly selective in the seasonings of sauces because I loathe disguising freshly produced food with innocuous versions of white, brown, or tomato sauces. The sauce should compliment the dish and not be the dominant feature. Generally speaking, a little bit goes a long way. Above all, it should be subtle.

I am sure you have seen, in the nether regions of food production, the cafeterias that range across the land from schools to multi-national companies where cheerful countermen pile glutinous masses of mystery sauces on top of over-cooked, wretched food. I am horrified at the growing tendency to use canned, condensed soups in recipes, as sauces. This is subordinating food preparation to the bureaucratic conveyor belt. Convenience foods will become the death knell of delicious, lovingly constructed meals.

The careful cooking of sauces is essential to the essence of appetizing meals.

Italian cooking is synonymous with tomato sauce. I will begin here with a short variety of tomato-based sauces, but will go on to include the others that give pasta such versatility as a food.

Basic Tomato Sauce 1 (Marinara Sauce)

$\frac{1}{3}$ *cup* (79 *ml.*) *olive oil*
3 *cloves garlic*
$\frac{1}{3}$ *cup* 75 *g.*) *chopped parsley*
$\frac{1}{2}$ *tsp.* (2.5 *g.*) *pepper*
2 *lb.* (900 *g.*) *fresh tomatoes, skinned*
1 *tsp.* (5 *g.*) *oregano*
$\frac{1}{2}$ *tsp.* (2.5 *g.*) *salt*

Gently brown the garlic cloves in the olive oil. Cut the tomatoes into quarters and add to the olive oil with the remaining seasonings. Stir slowly, breaking the tomatoes into smaller pieces. Cook slowly for 10 minutes.

Basic Tomato Sauce 2

1 *lb.* (454 *g.*) *freshly skinned tomatoes*
 or 2 (16 *oz.* or 450 *g.*) *cans Italian plum tomatoes*
1 *tbsp.* (14 *g.*) *salt*
1 *tbsp.* (14 *g.*) *freshly ground pepper*
½ *tsp.* (2.5 *g.*) *sugar*
fresh parsley
2 (6 *oz.* or 170 *g.*) *cans tomato paste*
3 *cloves garlic*
¼ *cup* (58 *ml.*) *olive oil*
6 *fresh basil leaves*
 or 1 *tsp.* (5 *g.*) *dried basil*

Pour the olive oil into a heavy skillet covering the bottom of the pan. Sauté the garlic to flavor the oil. Cut the tomatoes into smaller pieces. If you are using canned tomatoes, squeeze out some of the juice with your hand. Add the tomatoes, salt, pepper, and sugar to the olive oil and garlic. Stir and break up the tomatoes with a wooden spoon. Blend in the tomato paste plus 2 cans water. Add the sweet basil and stir frequently for 5 minutes, until the sauce begins to thicken. Do not over-cook—20 minutes is sufficient time for this sauce. Do not overload your taste buds with onions, carrots or other ingredients. Then it becomes another sauce. (This sauce is especially good when tomatoes are in season. The variations are endless with the addition of fish, other herbs, meat.)

Basic Meat Sauce 1

Many years ago, my mother explained the secret of her consistently wonderful meat sauce: always use a bit of lean pork and a smidge of sugar for canned tomatoes.

2 (*approx.* 12 *oz.* or 340 *g.*) *cans tomatoes or tomato purée*
3 *cloves garlic*
1 *tsp.* (5 *g.*) *sugar*
1 (6 *oz.* or 170 *g.*) *can tomato paste*
salt
black pepper
¼ *tsp.* (1.25 *g.*) *red pepper*
sweet basil
1 *lb.* (454 *g.*) *lean hamburger*
water
olive oil
oregano
¼ *lb.* (114 *g.*) *lean pork*

Cover the bottom of the pan with olive oil. Add the garlic and gently cook for a minute. Add the tomato paste and one can full of water. Stir until blended. Add the canned tomatoes and seasonings and mix thoroughly before adding the meat. Stir the meat into the sauce and turn the heat very low. Let the sauce bubble and cook, stirring from time to time, for 2 hours. Remove extra fat that rises to the surface, with the spoon. It will thicken gradually until about a third of the liquid has disappeared. It is now done.

Succulent Sauces (*overleaf page* 140)
Marinara sauce, meat sauce, olive oil and garlic sauce, and béchamel sauce are the bases of many recipes.
Spaghetti with Marinara Sauce (*overleaf page* 141)
Fresh tomatoes and olive oil make a most simple spaghetti dish which can be cooked in minutes and is recommended as a simple health food with low fat content.

Mom's Spaghetti Sauce with Meatballs

1 (6 oz. or 170 g.) can tomato paste
1 (16 oz. or 450 g.) can tomatoes
2 cloves garlic, finely chopped
4 basil leaves or dried basil
2 tbsp. (30 ml.) olive oil
1 (15 oz. or 420 g.) can tomato sauce
small piece of bay leaf
¼ cup (55 g.) chopped parsley
salt and pepper
¾ lb. (340 g.) pork butt

Cook tomato paste in oil, stirring constantly. Add one can of water, tomato sauce, and tomatoes, mashed. Add the garlic, salt, pepper, pinch sugar, bay leaf, parsley, basil and pork butt. Cook slowly for 1 hour. Add the meatballs and cook for half-an-hour longer. Add water if it thickens too much.

Meatballs:
⅔ lb. (300 g.) ground beef
⅓ lb. (150 g.) ground pork
3 slices hard bread, soaked in water
2 tbsp. (30 ml.) oil
¼ cup (55 g.) parmesan cheese
2 eggs
2 tsp. (10 g.) chopped parsley
1 tsp. (5 g.) garlic powder
½ tsp. (2.5 g.) salt

Squeeze out the water from the bread and add to the ground meat in a bowl. Break the eggs into the bowl and add cheese, parsley, garlic powder and salt. Mix the meat and eggs with your hands; when it is completely blended take about 2 tablespoons (30 grams) into your hand and roll into a ball. Fry in hot oil until browned on all sides. Remove from the pan, drain and add to the meat sauce.

For those of you who do not have Italian Sausage available:

Homemade Italian Sausage

1 pork butt (3-4 lb. or 1.4-1.8 kg.) ground
½ cup (112 g.) salt
2 tbsp. (28 g.) freshly ground pepper
2 tbsp. (28 g.) fennel seed
⅓ lb. (150 g.) pork casings (either frozen or from the butcher)
2 tsp. (10 g.) crushed red pepper
¼ cup (55 g.) paprika

Have the butcher grind the pork butt. If it is too lean add a bit more fat. Flatten the meat out on a board or Formica-topped table. Sprinkle the salt, black pepper, red pepper, fennel seed and paprika evenly over the top of the meat. Mix the seasonings and meat with your fingers; it is easier to stuff the sausage meat into the casings if it is chilled. The sausage meat will keep uncooked for ten days in the refrigerator. I usually sauté some sausage meat down, just to add to sauce or other dishes.

Spaghetti with Sausage

1½ lb. (680 g.) Italian sausage (mix sweet with hot)
2 tbsp. (30 ml.) olive oil

Follow the basic Tomato Sauce recipe (p. 138). Cook the sausage in the olive oil, slowly. Turn so that the sausage is brown on all sides and add to the tomato sauce and cook for 1 hour, over a low heat.

Mom's Holiday or Sunday Lunch (Braciola, Pepertoni and Pork Loin)

Basic Tomato Sauce (p. 138)
¾ lb. (340 g.) lean pork loin
2 Braciola
1 Pepertoni

Add the pork loin to the sauce and cook for half-an-hour. Meanwhile, make the Pepertoni and Braciola:

Pepertoni:
(large meat loaf with sausage)
1 10-inch (25 cm.) hot Italian sausage link
⅔ lb. (300 g.) ground beef
⅓ lb. (150 g.) ground pork
3 slices hard bread soaked in water
½ tsp. (2.5 g.) salt
¼ cup (55 g.) parmesan cheese
2 eggs
2 tsp. (10 g.) chopped parsley
1 tsp. (5 g.) garlic powder
2 tbsp. (30 ml.) olive oil

Mix the eggs, cheese, salt, parsley, garlic powder and pour over the ground meat. Squeeze the water from the bread and add to the mixture. Mix with your hands until the meat is blended with the other ingredients. Flatten out the meat mixture with the palm of your hand. Lay the sausage on one side and fold over. Pinch the edges to seal.

Momma's (Braciola) Rolled Meat:
¾ lb. (340 g.) round steak cut very thin
1 egg
¼ cup (55 g.) parmesan cheese
2 tbsp. (30 ml.) olive oil
2 tbsp. (28 g.) chopped parsley
½ tsp. (2.5 g.) garlic powder
¼ cup (55 g.) soft breadcrumbs

Mix the egg, cheese, parsley, garlic powder and bread-crumbs in a bowl. Flatten out the round steak and cut into two. Lay a piece of waxed paper over the top and pound with the flat side of a meat cleaver. Remove the wax paper; spread the egg mixture on the steak and roll up like a jelly-roll and tie with string, or you can use sturdy tooth-picks. Brown in the olive oil and drain.

Add the pepertoni and braciola to the tomato sauce and cook slowly for 1 hour. Serve the pork, pepertoni and braciola sliced on a warm platter with additional sauce. I usually serve the spaghetti first with just the sauce and parmesan cheese. Then, as a separate course accompanied by a large mixed green salad, I serve the meat.

Braciola with Eggs and Ham in Sauce

1½ lb. (680 g.) round steak
2 tbsp. (28 g.) parsley
2 slices parma ham
½ tsp. (2.5 g.) salt
½ cup (118 ml.) white wine
¼ cup (58 ml.) melted butter
2 cloves garlic, minced
½ cup (112 g.) parmesan cheese
½ cup (112 g.) fresh breadcrumbs
2 eggs, hard boiled
½ tsp. (2.5 g.) crushed red pepper
1 (16 oz. or 450 g.) can tomatoes
2 (6 oz. or 170 g.) cans tomato paste
¼ cup (58 ml.) olive oil
¼ cup (55 g.) pine nuts or raisins
pinch oregano
pinch sugar

Pound the round steak under waxed paper. Mix the parsley, breadcrumbs, minced garlic, pine nuts, salt and pepper in a bowl. Add the melted butter until the breadcrumbs are moist. Remove the waxed paper from the meat and lay the parma ham across the meat. Slice the hard boiled eggs and arrange. Add the breadcrumb mixture over the top. Roll up the meat like a jelly-roll and then tie with string. Heat the olive oil and brown the Braciola on all sides. Add the tomatoes, tomato paste, water, white wine, herbs and seasoning. Cook till the meat is tender, approximately 1½–2 hours. Add more water if the sauce becomes too thick. Serve over spaghetti.

Sunday Lunch (*overleaf*)
Spaghetti with meat sauce followed by pepertoni and braciola was our traditional midday meal on Sundays.

Stuffed Roll of Veal

1½ lb. (680 g.) veal round
4 slices prosciutto ham
¼ cup (55 g.) parmesan cheese
1 cup (225 g.) sliced mushrooms
1 clove garlic, mashed
2 tbsp. (28 g.) parsley chopped
¼ cup (55 g.) butter
1 cup (237 ml.) beef broth
¼ cup (58 ml.) olive oil
2 tbsp. (28 g.) flour
½ tsp. (2.5 g.) salt
1 cup (237 ml.) wine
1 tsp. (5 g.) black pepper

Pound the veal under waxed paper. Arrange the ham on the veal and cover with parmesan cheese and parsley. Roll up like a jelly-roll and tie. Brown the veal in the olive oil on all sides. Remove the veal. In a saucepan melt the butter in the oil. Scrape all the scraps from the sides of the veal pan into the mixture and slowly add the flour until smooth. Add the beef broth gradually so the sauce remains smooth. Add the wine, garlic, seasoning and mushrooms. Return the veal roll to the sauce and simmer for 1 hour. Add more water if the sauce is too thick. Slice the roll and arrange over a platter of cooked, drained noodles. Spoon the sauce over the top.

Tomato Sauce and Pork Chops

6 large pork chops with kidney
1 (28 oz. or 780 g.) can tomatoes
1 (6 oz. or 170 g.) can tomato paste and water
pinch oregano
pinch rosemary
2 cloves garlic
¼ cup (55 g.) chopped parsley
1 tsp. (5 g.) sugar
4 sweet basil leaves
1 tsp. (5 g.) salt
1 tsp. (5 g.) red crushed pepper
¼ cup (58 ml.) olive oil

Brown the pork chops lightly in the olive oil and remove. Add the tomatoes, tomato paste and 1 can of water to the pot. Stir in all the bits clinging to the bottom of the pan. Put in the garlic, oregano, rosemary, parsley, sweet basil leaves, salt, sugar and crushed red pepper into the sauce. Stir for a few minutes and then return the pork chops to the pan and simmer in the tomato sauce for 1 hour.

Meat Sauce 2

1 lb. (454 g.) ground lamb or venison
½ lb. (227 g.) ground pork
¼ cup (58 ml.) olive oil
1 onion, minced
2 cloves garlic
2 tsp. (10 g.) freshly chopped parsley
1 tsp. (5 g.) oregano
4 sweet basil leaves
1 tsp. (5 g.) parmesan cheese
½ cup (118 ml.) white wine
2 (6 oz. or 170 g.) cans tomato paste
1 cup (237 ml.) water
pinch of sugar
pinch of crushed red pepper
½ tsp. (2.5 g.) salt
½ tsp. (2.5 g.) freshly ground black pepper
1 (28 oz. or 780 g.) can tomatoes

In a large pot sauté the onions and garlic in the olive oil. Add the tomato paste and water, blending until smooth. Squeeze the water from the tomatoes and add to the mixture. Put in the parsley, sweet basil, salt, cheese, black pepper, red pepper and sugar. Stir. Add the wine. When the sauce begins to bubble sprinkle the ground meat into the pan. Stir and gently cook, uncovered for 45 minutes.

Bolognese Sauce (Ragout)

Probably the name 'Bolognese Sauce' has misled many diners into thinking that the tomato/meat mixture they are consuming is authentic. A true Bolognese Sauce has little tomato but depends upon cooked vegetables for its unique flavor.

½ cup (112 g.) butter
½ lb. (227 g.) ground beef
6 chicken livers
4 oz. (112 g.) thick-cut unsmoked bacon, diced
2 carrots
1 large onion, sliced
stalk celery
2 tsp. (10 g.) parmesan cheese
4 tbsp. (60 ml.) tomato paste
½ cup (118 ml.) white wine
1 cup (237 ml.) beef stock
½ tsp. (2.5 g.) nutmeg
1 bay leaf
1 tsp. (5 g.) freshly ground black pepper
½ tsp. (2.5 g.) salt

Clean and remove the green sac from the livers. Cut into small pieces. Cut the bacon and salt pork into small pieces; chop the carrots, onion and celery. In a heavy pot, sauté the bacon until brown in the butter. Add the carrots, onions, celery and continue cooking until they are brown. Add the ground beef, stirring until it loses its redness then add the tomato paste, white wine and stock. Cook for 10 minutes then add the chopped liver, nutmeg, ground pepper and salt. Cover tightly and simmer for 40 minutes. Pour over green noodles or lasagne verdi and serve with parmesan cheese.

Chicken in Sauce

2 *large breasts of chicken cut in half*
2 *legs of chicken*
2 *thighs of chicken*
1 *(28 oz. or 780 g.) can tomatoes*
2 *(6 oz. or 170 g.) cans tomato paste*
3 *cloves garlic*
¼ *cup (55 g.) butter*
4 *fresh basil leaves*
1 *tsp. (5 g.) salt*
1 *tsp. (5 g.) freshly ground pepper*
pinch of red pepper
1 *cup (237 ml.) white wine*
¼ *cup (58 ml.) olive oil*
1 *tsp. (5 g.) rosemary*

Wash and dry the chicken pieces; melt the butter in the olive oil and brown the chicken on all sides. Remove. Add the tomato paste and wine. Stir all the bits and pieces into the sauce and add the tomatoes, crushing with a wooden spoon. Add the garlic cloves, rosemary, basil, salt and black pepper and red pepper. Stir well and cook till the sauce begins to bubble. Return the chicken to the sauce. Cook slowly for 1 hour but be careful not to overcook.

Eggplant and Sausage Sauce

1 *large eggplant (aubergine)*
1 *lb. (454 g.) Italian sausage meat*
¼ *cup (58 ml.) olive oil*
3 *cloves garlic, minced*
2 *onions, diced*
2 *tbsp. (28 g.) fresh parsley*
1 *tsp. (5 g.) black pepper*
1 *tsp. (5 g.) salt*
½ *cup (118 ml.) white wine*
5 *large tomatoes*

Wash and cut the eggplant into small cubes; place in salted water while you prepare the remainder of the sauce Blanch and skin 5 large, juicy tomatoes and cut into small pieces. If the sausage is in a casing, split the casing down the center of the sausage and remove the meat. In a heavy pot sauté the garlic and the onions until golden. Add the sausage meat, cooking gently, until the color turns. Drain and dry the eggplant. Put into the pan with the sausage and gently cook for 10 minutes. Add the tomatoes, white wine, black pepper, salt and parsley. Stir until blended and cook for 40 minutes, over a low heat.

Rabbit in Sauce
(Also Goat and Venison)

Cook the same way as Chicken in Sauce above with the following exception: before removing the browned rabbit from the skillet, pour ½ cup (120 ml.) brandy over it and light with a match. Let it simmer until the flame disappears, then remove the rabbit. Carry on with the sauce. This recipe is also excellent with goat meat and venison.

The Tra La La Sauce (Italian Meat Sauce)

This is a recipe from Mrs. Tartaglia in Utica, New York.

1 lb. (454 g.) spare ribs
1 lb. (454 g.) hot sausage
1 lb. (454 g.) beef (in one piece)
¼ cup (58 ml.) olive oil
1 large (28 oz. or 780 g.) can tomatoes
1 (15 oz. or 450 ml.) can tomato sauce
1 (6 oz. or 170 g.) can tomato paste
1½ tsp. (7.5 g.) salt
¼ tsp. (1.25 g.) black pepper
2 basil leaves

Put oil in frying pan or Dutch oven with 2 cloves garlic and half an onion. Brown the meat. When browned, remove from pan and set aside. In the pan, put in the tomatoes, sauce and paste and 2 cups (450 ml.) of water. Let cook for 1½ hours. Put in your meat and let it cook for an hour more. Serve over your favorite pasta.

Tuna Fish Balls and Tomato Sauce

2 (6 oz. or 170 g.) cans tuna fish
2 tbsp. (28 g.) onions, minced
1 egg
½ cup (112 g.) fresh breadcrumbs
¼ cup (58 ml.) olive oil
1 (28 oz. or 780 g.) can tomatoes
1 tbsp. (14 g.) fresh parsley
4 leaves sweet basil
¼ cup (58 ml.) white wine
½ tsp. (2.5 g.) pepper
½ tsp. (2.5 g.) salt

In a small bowl mix the tuna fish, minced onion, egg, breadcrumbs and parsley. Roll small balls in you hand. Heat the olive oil and fry the tuna balls until brown on all sides. Remove. Add the tomatoes to the oil, crushing them with your spoon. Blend in the wine, sweet basil, salt and pepper and cook for one half-hour, adding water if the sauce becomes too thick. Return the tuna balls to the sauce and cook for another 15–20 minutes. Delicious over spaghetti.

Lamb Shanks and Tomato Sauce

4 large lamb (or veal) shanks
½ cup (112 g.) flour
¼ cup (58 ml.) olive oil
¼ cup (55 g.) butter
1 (16 oz. or 450 g.) can tomatoes
3 cloves garlic
½ tsp. (2.5 g.) salt
½ tsp. (2.5 g.) crushed red pepper
½ cup (118 ml.) white wine
1 cup (237 ml.) chicken broth
1 bay leaf
1 tsp. (5 g.) thyme
1 tsp. (5 g.) rosemary
1 apple
2 onions
1 tbsp. (14 g.) hot curry powder

In a large heavy pan, melt the butter in the olive oil and sauté the garlic cloves. Dredge the lamb shanks in the flour and brown on all sides in the olive oil. Remove. Add the tomatoes, salt, red pepper, wine, chicken broth, bay leaf, thyme and rosemary. Stir until the ingredients are blended. Peel and quarter the apple and onions. Add to the sauce with the curry powder. Return the lamb shanks to the sauce and cook over a low heat, stirring occasionally for an hour. Remove the shanks. Whisk the sauce until blended. Return the shanks to the sauce. Excellent served with wide noodles.

Veal Shanks and Spaghetti
Economical and hearty—a perfect winter's meal.

148

Beef Shanks with Tomato Sauce

1 cup (225 g.) flour
4 large beef shanks (2 inch or 5 cm.)
1 (6 oz. or 200 g.) can tomato paste
1 onion, minced
2 cups (475 ml.) beef broth
3 cloves garlic, minced
¼ cup (58 ml.) olive oil
salt and pepper
½ cup (118 ml.) red wine (dry)
1 tsp. (5 g.) thyme
1 tsp. (5 g.) rosemary
4 anchovy fillets
1 tbsp. (14 g.) parsley
1 tbsp. (14 g.) lemon rind
1 tbsp. (14 g.) minced garlic
pinch crushed red pepper

Dredge the meat in flour. In a large skillet braise the beef shanks on all sides. Add the beef broth, tomato paste, wine, onion, garlic, thyme, rosemary and anchovy fillets. Simmer for 2 hours or until the meat is tender. Add more wine if the sauce becomes too thick. When the meat is cooked, arrange on a platter of wide, cooked and buttered noodles. Cover with the sauce. Mix the parsley, lemon rind and garlic. Sprinkle over the top of the dish before serving.

Ruth's Spaghetti Sauce with Sausage

My sister-in-law was born in Germany and is an excellent cook. This is her adaptation of the 'family' recipe. It is delicious.

1 (2 lb. 3 oz. or 1 kg.) can tomatoes
2 (15 oz. or 450 g.) cans tomato sauce
2 (6 oz. or 170 g.) cans tomato paste
1 tsp. (5 g.) Italian seasoning
½ cup (112 g.) parmesan cheese
2 lb. (1 kg.) Italian sausage
2 cups (475 ml.) water
1 tsp. (5 g.) sugar
salt
2–3 cloves garlic (crushed)
3–4 leaves sweet basil

Mix all the ingredients except the sausage. Fry the sausage until lightly brown and add to the sauce. Cook for 2 hours.

White Clam Sauce

¼ cup (58 ml.) olive oil
1 clove garlic
¼ cup (58 ml.) water
½ tsp. (2.5 g.) chopped parsley
½ tsp. (2.5 g.) salt
¼ tsp. (1.25 g.) oregano
¼ tsp. (1.25 g.) pepper (black)
1 can minced clams plus juice

Brown garlic in oil, then add water and other ingredients, adding clams last. Simmer about 15 minutes. Pour over linguine or spaghetti.

Anchovy Sauce

8 *tbsp.* (112 *g.*) *unsalted butter*
¼ *cup* (55 *g.*) *chopped parsley*
salt and pepper
1 *can anchovy fillets, finely chopped*
2 *tbsp.* (30 *ml.*) *lemon juice*

Melt butter and stir in anchovies, parsley, lemon juice and spices to taste. Pour over cooked linguine.

Oil and Garlic Sauce

½ *cup* (118 *ml.*) *olive oil*
½ *cup* (118 *ml.*) *water*
½ *tsp.* (2.5 *g.*) *black or red pepper*
3 *cloves garlic, slivered*
1 *tbsp.* (14 *g.*) *chopped parsley*

Brown garlic in oil. Add other ingredients and simmer about 15 minutes. Pour over linguine or spaghetti.

HEALTH FOOD PASTA

Many of the recipes that included vegetables, fish and lean meat in the preceding chapters are basically health food dishes. Spinach macaroni and noodles of course have more nutrients than the basic semolina pasta. In recent years as we became aware of the danger of eating an overly refined diet, certain 'health' foods were especially packaged to help maintain a suitable level of bran and wheat germ intake into our diets. Among these products were germ-based macaroni made from stone-milled whole-wheat flour. Buckwheat spaghetti and whole-wheat pasta shapes are available in specialized shops.

Do not let the dark brown color put you off. The taste of the spaghetti is nutty and full-bodied. The Japanese use a similarly based spaghetti served cold with a soy sauce as an appetizer. I perused many 'health food' cookbooks and found the majority of recipes were variations based on cheese—not very imaginative and certainly not complementing the basic flavor of the whole-wheat flour. Strongly flavored vegetables, fish and pungent sauces enhance the basic taste of the whole-wheat pasta. Remember, the essence of any concept of 'health food' is to use pure, unrefined products. Seed and nut oils have more food value than pure vegetable oils. I add olive oil in certain recipes to the seed oil when I think the blend will enhance the flavor. Health food seasonings should not be bland—add herbs, soy sauce, mustard, sea salt mixed with sesame and yeast mixtures to your sauces to complement the taste of the vegetable or protein mixture you are preparing. Any product containing whole-wheat germ needs to be refrigerated to retain the taste and freshness. It will go off if not kept in a cool atmosphere. Be careful when you purchase commercial whole-wheat spaghetti that it has not been sitting on the shelf for an extended period. Health food need not be the medicinally bland diet that many non-converts expect when self-righteously eating the 'proper' foods.

The following are recipes I have developed in my kitchen which are delicious as well as nutritious.

Basic Homemade Whole-Wheat Pasta

4 *cups* (900 g.) *whole-wheat flour*
1 *tbsp.* (15 ml.) *olive oil*
3 *eggs*
¼ *cup* (58 ml.) *water*

Follow the general instructions for making pasta dough (p. 26). Be careful with the water—you may not need the whole amount. I find the dough is easier to roll if chilled for an hour in the refrigerator.

Eggplant and Chicken Lasagne

Use the basic whole-wheat pasta dough and roll out paper thin and cut into lasagne strips. Cook for 5 minutes and drain on a tea cloth.

Sauce:

1 *eggplant (aubergine), diced*
2 *tomatoes, diced*
1 *onion, diced*
2 *cloves garlic*
1 *tsp.* (5 g.) *sea salt*
½ *lb.* (227 g.) *mozzarella*
2 *tbsp.* (30 ml.) *seed oil*
½ *tsp.* (2.5 g.) *sweet basil*
1 *tsp.* (5 g.) *rosemary*
¼ *cup* 58 ml.) *chicken broth*
2 *cups* (450 g.) *sliced chicken*

Gently steam the vegetables in the chicken broth. Add the oil and seasonings. Arrange a layer of the lasagne in the bottom of a casserole, spoon the sauce over the pasta; arrange the slices of chicken on top. Continue with the layering until you have filled the casserole. End with the eggplant sauce. Dot with mozzarella and bake for 40 minutes in a moderate oven. Cool for 20 minutes and serve.

Two Cheese Whole-Wheat Spaghetti

1 *lb.* (454 g.) *whole-wheat spaghetti*
½ *lb.* (227 g.) *ricotta*
½ *lb.* (227 g.) *mozzarella*
¼ *cup* (58 ml.) *seed-based oil (sunflower)*
2 *tbsp.* (30 ml.) *olive oil*
2 *cloves garlic*
¼ *cup* (55 g.) *chopped parsley*
1 *tsp.* (5 g.) *sea salt and sesame seed seasoning*
1 *tsp.* (5 g.) *fresh, sweet basil*
½ *tsp.* (2.5 g.) *freshly ground pepper*

In a skillet, brown the garlic in the oil until just soft. Add the seasonings. Cook the spaghetti until *al dente*. Drain to a hot platter. Spoon the ricotta and mozzarella over the spaghetti. Pour over the olive oil mixture and toss. Serve immediately.

Cabbage and Tomato Spaghetti

2 tbsp. (30 ml.) seed oil
2 cloves garlic
½ head savoy cabbage, shredded
1 lb. (454 g.) wholemeal spaghetti
3 tomatoes, skinned
2 tsp. (10 g.) fennel seed
½ tsp. (2.5 g.) crushed red pepper
1 tsp. (5 g.) sea salt

In a saucepan combine the garlic, cabbage, tomatoes and seasonings with the oil. Steam until the vegetables are crunchy. Cook the spaghetti until *al dente*. Drain to a platter and spoon the mixture over the top of the pasta. Serve hot.

Eggplant and Pepper Bake

½ lb. (227 g.) short-cut macaroni
1 eggplant (aubergine), diced
2 green peppers, diced
1 tsp. (5 g.) sea salt
¼ cup (58 ml.) seed oil
2 cloves garlic
2 tsp. (2.5 g.) oregano
2 sprigs parsley
2 tomatoes, skinned
1 onion, cut into slices
½ tsp. (2.5 g.) fennel seed
2 sprigs parsley
1 tsp. (5 g.) honey
¼ cup (55 g.) parmesan cheese
4 slices mozzarella

Cook the macaroni until *al dente*. In a saucepan sauté the garlic, chopped tomatoes and peppers, until soft. Meanwhile, place the eggplant in salted water, drain and add to the saucepan. Add the seasonings and cook for a few minutes but do not over-cook. Arrange a layer of the drained macaroni in the bottom of a buttered casserole. Pour some sauce over the top. Sprinkle with parmesan cheese. Continue layering until you end up with the eggplant mixture on top. Dot with mozzarella cheese. Bake in a moderate (350°) oven for 30 minutes and serve hot.

Whole-Wheat Cannelloni

Use the basic whole-wheat recipe for pasta dough. Roll out in a thin sheet and cut into 3 by 4 inch (7.6 by 10 cm.) rectangles. Cook until *al dente* and drain to a tea towel.

Stuffing:
½ cup (112 g.) minced chicken
½ cup (112 g.) eggplant (aubergine), diced
½ cup (112 g.) mushrooms
1 tsp. (5 g.) sea salt
1 garlic clove, crushed
2 tomatoes, skinned and diced
1 tsp. (5 g.) oregano
3 basil leaves
1 tbsp. (15 ml.) seed oil
1 cup (237 ml.) chicken broth

In a pan, sauté the garlic, diced tomato, diced eggplant, mushrooms, ¼ cup (60 ml.) of the broth and seasonings. Cook until soft. Add the chicken. Mix thoroughly. Arrange 2 teaspoons (10 grams) on each pasta rectangle and roll. Arrange in a greased baking dish. Cover with remaining broth and bake for 20 minutes at 375° and serve.

Spinach and Chicken Wholemeal Spaghetti

1 lb. (454 g.) fresh spinach
1 cup (237 ml.) bouillon
½ cup (112 g.) sliced chicken
½ tsp. (2.5 g.) nutmeg
1 lb. (454 g.) wholemeal spaghetti
½ tsp. (2.5 g.) sea salt

Bring the bouillon to a boil. Add the spinach, cover tightly and remove from the heat. Cook the spaghetti until *al dente* and drain to a warm bowl. Quickly add the chicken and seasonings to the spinach. Heat. Arrange the spinach on top of the spaghetti, spoon the chicken and broth over the top. The essence of this dish is the spinach. Do not overcook. It should still be bright green and crunchy.

Fennel, Beef and Soy Sauce

Sauce:

½ cup (118 ml.) soy sauce
¼ cup (58 ml.) honey
¼ cup (58 ml.) rice wine (sake)
1 cup (225 g.) bamboo shoots
½ lb. (227 g.) mushrooms
2 large fennel bulbs
½ lb. (227 g.) lean beef thinly cut
1 lb. (454 g.) whole-wheat spaghetti

In a saucepan mix the soy sauce, honey and rice wine. Cut the fennel into cubes (including the fern) and gently cook until *al dente*. Cook the spaghetti and drain to a bowl. Quickly add the meat, mushrooms and bamboo shoots to the sauce. Spoon the mixture over the spaghetti and toss. Serve hot.

The above recipe can be varied with the following combinations using the basic soy sauce.
1. Bean sprouts, water chestnuts, mushrooms and spring onions
2. Green peppers and sliced chicken or lean beef

Wine and Chestnut Sauce

2 cups (450 g.) blanched, cooked chestnuts
1 cup (237 ml.) white wine
2 tbsp. (30 ml.) seed oil
1 tbsp. (28 g.) bran flour
3 sprigs parsley
1 tsp. (5 g.) sea salt
½ tsp. (2.5 g.) marjoram
1 lb. (454 g.) buckwheat spaghetti

In a saucepan blend the flour with the oil until smooth. Slowly add the wine, stirring continuously. Add the chestnuts and cook for 10 minutes until the sauce has thickened. Add the seasonings. Cook the spaghetti until *al dente*. Arrange on the platter and spoon the chestnut sauce over the top. Garnish with parsley and serve.

Chestnuts and Mushrooms in Wine Sauce over Whole-Wheat Spaghetti
Bursting with nutrition, a health-food pasta dish for the most discerning gourmet.

Cauliflower (or Broccoli) Cheese

½ lb. (227 g.) short-cut whole-wheat macaroni
1 cup (237 ml.) non-fat milk
½ cup (112 g.) grated cheese
2 tbsp. (28 g.) whole-wheat flour
3 tbsp. (45 ml.) seed oil
1 cauliflower, cooked in sea salt and sesame seed oil
1 tsp. (5 g.) sea salt and sesame seed
½ tsp. (2.5 g.) thyme
1 tsp. (5 g.) mustard
1 tomato, skinned
¼ cup (55 g.) fresh wholemeal breadcrumbs
garlic
parsley

Cook the pasta until *al dente*. In a saucepan blend the flour and oil until smooth. Gradually add the milk to the mixture stirring until blended. Crush the tomato and add. Cook for 5 minutes; add the seasonings and cheese. Cook till the cheese has melted. In a greased casserole arrange a layer of macaroni, cheese sauce and mashed cauliflower. Continue layering until you have filled the bowl. Mix the wholemeal breadcrumbs, minced garlic, parsley and oil in a bowl. Sprinkle over the top of the macaroni and bake for 30 minutes until brown on top.

Cod Fish and Tomato Bake

½ lb. (227 g.) short-cut macaroni
½ lb. (227 g.) cooked cod fish
4 tomatoes, sliced
½ cup (118 ml.) chicken bouillon
½ cup (118 ml.) tomato juice
1 tsp. (5 g.) oregano
1 tsp. (5 g.) sweet basil
1 tsp. (5 g.) parsley
2 cloves garlic, crushed
1 tsp. (5 g.) salt

Combine the seasonings in a bowl. Cook the macaroni until *al dente* and drain. Pour the macaroni in the bottom of a greased baking dish. Arrange the cooked fish over the macaroni, sprinkle the seasoning over the fish and place the slices of tomato on top. Pour the tomato juice and bouillon over the mixture and bake for 30 minutes. Serve hot.

SOUPS

We have never been a sandwich-eating family; if we have a hearty lunch then we usually have a thick soup and salad for supper. I normally keep a large variety of processed foods in the cupboard to supplement soups that need extending. I make a basic stock once a week from either a boiling fowl or meat bones. Ribs from the left-over Sunday roast or leg of lamb are ideal for this purpose. The stock can then be used for soups and sauces. Since our family has dwindled to two, now that our daughter has departed for university and the joys of maturity, we no longer feed an army of teenagers —a race which soon scents the home with the most interesting refrigerator and descends on it in hordes to fill its bottomless pits. Nonetheless, I still set aside measured quantities of the stock and freeze them for our use or for the unexpected guest. Be sure to label the packets' contents, quantity and date, however. Forethought does not then turn into frustration and mistakes.

If your family is like ours you usually have people popping in for lunch or staying beyond cocktails for dinner. Left-overs in the fridge are the greatest source of inspiration for a quick soup. All those little saran-wrapped dishes that contain remnants from forgotten meals combined with a frozen stock perhaps extended with mushrooms or fish from the store cupboard become a hearty soup with the addition of pasta. Soups of this type are great fun to make. Following are recipes for soups that have evolved from the refrigerator/cupboard syndrome, or are traditional soups that have been family recipes for many years. I have adapted some of our traditional recipes to my family's taste.

Basic Soup Stocks

Rich Beef Stock:
1/4 lb. (114 g.) salt pork
2 large carrots, sliced into 1 inch (2.5 cm.) pieces
2 stalks celery, including leaves
10 peppercorns
1½ lb. (680 g.) stewing beef*
1/4 cup (55 g.) chopped fresh parsley
½ tsp. (2½ g.) crushed red pepper
2 onions, cut into quarters
1 other seasonal root vegetable (turnip, parsnip, rutabaga)
1 tbsp. (14 g.) salt
3 quarts (2.8 liters) cold water
1 bay leaf
1 clove garlic

*Shank with the bones, or ask your butcher to cut you a marrow bone into 2 inch (5 cm.) pieces and add the stewing beef.

Bring the bones to a boil and then strain. Place the remaining ingredients into a large soup pot with fresh, cold water. Put the rinsed bones into the pot and gently cook, barely bubbling, until the liquid has decreased by one-third. This will take approximately 2½–3 hours. When the stock is fully cooked, remove the meat bones and strain the broth. Mash or liquidize the pulp that is left and blend into the stock. I usually use the meat in the first soup I prepared from this stock. What is left is a highly concentrated stock for soups and/or sauces. Alternate the beef with lamb bones for a different flavor.

Rich Chicken Stock:
1 boiling fowl (2–3 lb. or 1 kg.)
3 onions
3 carrots
4 stalks celery
2 bay leaves
3 or 4 leeks
enough water to cover
10 black peppercorns
1 tbsp. (14 g.) salt
1 tbsp. (15 ml.) lemon juice
1 pinch rosemary
parsley
1 seasonal root vegetable (turnip, parsnip, rutabaga)

Wash and cut the chicken into quarters. I usually blanch the chicken, rinse and place into a large stock pot. Cut the vegetables into chunk-size pieces, add the water and seasonings. Generally speaking, I correct the stock for salt when it is finished cooking. It is easier, obviously, to put more salt in than to try to make a dish less salty. Cook the stock for 2 hours. Remove the chicken. You can use the boiled chicken in a variety of recipes—soups, with sauces, salads or in sandwiches. I usually place the cooked meat into labelled packages in the freezer for future use, according to size. Either place the cooked vegetables into a blender or mash with a fork so that the contents can either be a clear broth or a richer broth with the added vegetables.

For a quick soup you add 1 tablespoon (15 g.) of pastina to one cup (240 ml.) of broth and cook for 7 minutes. Add a few of the mashed vegetables (1 teaspoon or 5 grams) and you have an excellent broth.

Pasta e Fagioli and Minestrone

Pasta e fagioli and minestrone are two hearty soups straight from the Italian farmer's kitchen which have traveled extensively abroad. They are two of the most popular soups served today. Economical, filled with protein and minerals, these two soups attain gourmet heights with well-chosen vegetables and herbs. I have eaten both in Italian restaurants from Tokyo to Spain and they have varied in texture from a vegetable-laced bouillon with homemade lasagnette noodles at Ada's Restaurant Itallienne in Commaruga, Spain, to a hefty main course dish at Chez Franco's, London. They are two soups which make a splendid main course, followed by salad, Italian bread, cheese and fruit. A bottle of solid red wine served with the soup elevates either dish to become the Queen of the soup family.

Pasta and Fagioli 1 (Bean and Macaroni)

Soak overnight ½ lb. (227 g.) white kidney or haricot beans. In the morning, drain and place the beans in a stock pot with the following ingredients:

2 *inch* (5 *cm.*) *slice of salt pork*
1 *beef marrow bone*
1 (6 *oz.* or 170 *g.*) *can tomato paste*
2 *quarts* (2 *liters*) *water*

Cover and cook gently for 2 hours.

In a separate small pan, sauté 1 large, sliced onion and 2 cloves of garlic in 4 tablespoons (60 ml.) olive oil. When the onion and garlic are soft, add to the stock pot with 2 tablespoons (28 g.) of chopped parsley, 1 teaspoon (5 g.) oregano, ½ teaspoon (2.5 g.) crushed red pepper and 1 teaspoon (5 g.) salt. Twenty minutes before the beans are cooked add 1 cup (225 g.) ditali or elbow macaroni. Cook until tender. Serve with parmesan cheese. Slices of pepperoni or salami can be used to garnish the top.

Pasta and Fagioli 2

My cousin Marie Panella Jones sent me her recipe which uses a marinara sauce.

Cook ½ lb. (227 g.) white navy beans until tender. Add 1 cup (237 ml.) marinara sauce. Add ¼ lb. (114 g.) broken pieces of spaghetti or small pasta 15 minutes before serving. Cook until *al dente*.

Minestrone

This is a basic recipe for minestrone. You can add other vegetables in season. If you wish to make it a heartier soup, add chunks of left-over beef or slices of Italian Sausage. Your butcher usually stocks thick ribs of pork or spare ribs cut into small pieces.

1 *lb.* (454 *g.*) *dried white kidney beans*
1 *lb.* (454 *g.*) *salt pork and spare ribs*
3 *cloves garlic*
2 *onions*
4 *carrots*
3 *stalks celery or fennel*
1 *cup* (225 *g.*) *green beans*
6 *oz.* (170 *g.*) *short-cut macaroni*
1 *sprig fresh parsley*
3 *quarts* (2.8 *liters*) *salted water*
2 *tbsp.* (30 *ml.*) *olive oil*
4 *large potatoes*
sweet basil
½ *head savoy cabbage*
5 *fresh tomatoes*
½ *cup* (112 *g.*) *green peas*
salt and pepper

Soak the beans overnight. Drain and add 2 quarts (1.9 liters) salted water. Simmer for 1 hour. Dice meat and sauté the onions and garlic in the olive oil. Prepare your vegetables, cutting into bite-sized pieces and interesting shapes. Add the vegetables, meat and onions/garlic to the soup pot. Cook on a low heat for 1½ hours. Twenty minutes before ready to serve, add the macaroni. Add the peas and any other cooked vegetables just before serving. Serve with parmesan cheese and garlic bread.

Meatball, Spinach and Pasta Soup (*above*)
Simple and filling, this soup can be enjoyed at least once a week.

Onion Soup Catalan (*above right*)
A hearty, main course soup based on the traditional 'soup of the mountains' in Spain.

Meatball and Spinach Soup

1 *cup* (225 g.) *pastina*
1 *lb*. (454 g.) *fresh, washed spinach* (*other seasonal greens can be used*)
½ *cup* (112 g.) *fresh breadcrumbs*
¼ *cup* (55 g.) *freshly ground parmesan cheese*
2 *quarts* (2 *l*.) *beef stock*
¾ *lb*. (340 g.) *ground meat* (*beef, veal or pork*)
2 *eggs, beaten*
salt
crushed red pepper

Mix the meat, breadcrumbs, eggs and cheese in a small bowl. Add a pinch of red pepper and ½ tablespoon (7 g.) salt. Pick up about 1 teaspoon (5 g.) of the mixture and roll gently in your hands to form a small meatball. Set these aside. Bring the beef stock to a boil. Add the meatballs and gently cook for 20 minutes. Add the pastina and cook for a further 5 minutes. Serves 6.

Onion Soup Catalan

3 oz. (42 g.) soup pasta
1 quart (946 ml.) chicken broth
3 onions, sliced
2 tbsp. (30 ml.) olive oil
salt and pepper
2 tbsp. (28 g.) cheese
4 eggs

In a flat skillet, sauté the onions in the oil until golden. Add the stock and bring to a full boil. Add the soup pasta and cook for 5 minutes. Break the eggs into the pan and poach for a further 5 minutes. Remove from the flame. Arrange an egg in each bowl and pour the soup around the egg. Sprinkle with cheese and serve.

Chicken and Lemon Soup

1 quart (946 ml.) chicken broth
4 tbsp. (55 g.) crushed vermicelli
2 tbsp. (30 ml.) fresh lemon juice
1 tbsp. (14 g.) flour
1 tbsp. (14 g.) butter
½ cup (112 g.) chicken slices

Blend the flour and butter into a paste in the bottom of a soup pot. Add ½ cup (120 ml.) of the chicken broth gradually into the mixture until it begins to thicken. Add the remaining broth gradually, stirring continuously. Cook gently for 5 minutes over a low heat. Increase the heat until the broth is bubbling and add the vermicelli. It will take approximately 6 minutes for the pasta to cook. Stir in the sliced chicken and lemon juice. Serves 4.

Beef, Tomato and Macaroni Soup

3 quarts (2.8 liters) beef broth
2 cups (450 g.) peeled tomatoes
sweet basil
pinch of thyme
½ tsp. (2.5 g.) crushed red pepper
½ lb. (227 g.) cooked beef (or ground meat)
olive oil
1 cup (225 g.) short-cut macaroni
salt

If you do not have left-over beef then sauté ½ lb. (230 g.) ground beef in a stock pot. Add the broth and seasonings. Cut the tomatoes into small pieces and stir into the broth. Add the macaroni and cook for 12 minutes, gently stirring. This is a hearty supper soup. If unexpected company arrives, add a can of white kidney beans.

Chicken Broth with Egg and Cheese (Stracciatella alla Romana)

1 quart (946 ml.) chicken broth
8 oz. (227 g.) soup pasta
3 tbsp. (42 g.) grated cheese
salt and pepper
3 eggs, well beaten
1 clove garlic
pinch marjoram

This is a version of the ragged egg soup of Rome.

Bring the stock to a boil and add the macaroni, a few at a time, stirring vigorously. Lower the heat and gently cook—about 10 minutes. In a small bowl, mince the garlic, add the seasonings, cheese and beaten eggs. Whisk until thoroughly blended. When the macaroni is *al dente* blend the egg mixture into the boiling stock and stir quickly. Serve at once.

Ravioli in Broda

You will need 10–12 ravioli per soup plate. I prefer the chicken or pork stuffed ravioli if I am using chicken stock or a heartier meat—beef or lamb—if I am using beef stock.

3 pints (1.4 liters) stock
60 ravioli
chopped parsley
parmesan cheese

Gently cook the ravioli for 20 minutes in the broth. Serve with chopped parsley and cheese.

Cauliflower Soup

1 cup (225 g.) cooked ditali
2 onions
4 tbsp. (60 ml.) olive oil
1 cup (225 g.) cubed potatoes
salt and pepper
1 small head of cauliflower
1 tbsp. (14 g.) flour
1 tbsp. (14 g.) butter
1 quart (946 ml.) stock
1 tsp. (5 g.) nutmeg

This is a thick supper soup.

Gently sauté the onions in the olive oil until golden. Add the stock, potatoes, seasonings and gently cook for 10 minutes. While it is cooking, break the cauliflower into small florets. Add to the soup mixture. Blend the flour and butter into a soft paste. Add a bit of the broth until it becomes thin and add slowly to the soup, blending gently. Cook for 5 minutes until thickened. Garnish with fresh parsley or paprika.

Cabbage, Chicken and Tomato Soup

2 quarts (2 liters) rich chicken broth
½ head savoy cabbage, chopped
2 cups (450 g.) cooked chicken
4 large tomatoes or 1 (16 oz. or 450 g.) can tomatoes
sprig of fresh parsley
1 cup ziti macaroni broken into short lengths

Bring the chicken stock to a boil. Add the skinned, chopped tomatoes, cabbage and macaroni. Cook gently for 20 minutes until the macaroni and cabbage are tender. Add the cooked chicken. Sprinkle with fresh parsley and serve.

Lentil and Macaroni Soup

1 quart (946 ml.) beef stock
½ lb. (227 g.) lentils
either a ham bone or ¼ lb. (114 g.) salt pork
2 potatoes
1 tbsp. (14 g.) margarine
1 tbsp. (14 g.) flour
6 oz. (170 g.) macaroni
1 fennel, cut

Soak the lentils for 2 hours. Drain, rinse and place in the stock pot with salt pork and beef stock. Simmer for 2 hours. Add the chopped fennel and cook for ½ hour. Twenty minutes before you are ready to serve the soup, add the diced potato and macaroni. Add the flour and margarine after you have blended the two together to form a roux. Adjust the seasonings and serve. Excellent with herb-flavored croutons.

Lentil with Pasta

Add enough water to a pan to cover 1 lb. (450 g.) of lentils. Cook until the lentils are soft. Add 1 tsp. (5 g.) salt. Brown 3 cloves garlic in a saucepan with 1 tbsp. (15 ml.) olive oil. Then put in 1 (6 oz. or 170 g.) can tomato paste, cook about 10 minutes and then add the mixture to the lentils. Cook the ditalini (1 cup or 225 g.) and drain. Mix with the lentils. This is an excellent simple lentil dish.

Mary Brindisi, Utica, New York

165

Tortellini in Broda

For the dough:
8 oz. (225 g.) flour
2 eggs

Filling:
4 chicken livers, chopped
1 oz. (28 g.) uncooked smoked ham
fresh basil
pinch salt, pepper and nutmeg
2 oz. (55 g.) cooked chicken
1 egg
fresh parsley
1 tbsp. (14 g.) parmesan cheese

Soup:
1½ quarts (1.4 liters) chicken broth

Use the traditional method of making pasta. Place the flour on a large pastry board or marble-topped table. Make a well with your fingers and add the beaten eggs. Work the flour and eggs together gently with your fingers and knead (about 10 minutes). Rest the dough under a bowl. After you have mixed the ingredients together for the filling, roll the dough out on a floured board until you can see the grain of the wood/marble showing through. Cut into rounds with a small juice glass or 2-inch (5 cm.) cutter. Place a teaspoon (5 grams) of stuffing on each round. Fold the dough over the filling and press the dough together at the sides of the now semi-circle. Bring the two ends together at the center. It is easy if you use your index finger as a mould. This forms the shape of a naval or cocked hat. Cook the pasta in boiling stock until they rise to the top. Serve with parmesan cheese.

Tradition tells us that the shape of the tortellini represents a woman's navel. Many stories exist explaining the origin of the shape—one story being that a cook dreamed of Venus rising from the sea and he awoke, rushed to his kitchen and tried to recreate the beauty of her navel. A more mundane story centers around a simple love affair inspiring the shape. Whatever the story, the resulting shape is exquisite and is not only excellent in broda, but in a timbale—light to the taste and fit to grace the table of the most discerning gourmet. In many cities you can buy them uncooked, along with ravioli but I prefer to make my own.

Tortellini in Broda
Delicate twists of pasta stuffed with meat and cheese comprise an excellent choice as a first course followed by fish.

Pea and Macaroni Soup

1 *quart* (950 *ml.*) *chicken broth*
2 *cups* (450 *g.*) *cooked peas*
1 *cup* (225 *g.*) *short-cut macaroni*

Bring the broth to a boil and add the macaroni. Cook until tender and add the peas. Gently combine with a spoon and serve at once with parmesan cheese.

Onion, Potato and Macaroni Soup

1 *quart* (950 *ml.*) *chicken broth*
4 *large onions, cut into slices*
2 *leeks* (*well washed*)
2 *cloves garlic*
2 *tbsp.* (30 *ml.*) *olive oil*
4 *large potatoes, peeled*
1 *cup* (225 *g.*) *ditali or shells*
1 *carrot*
½ *cup* (112 *g.*) *white beans* (*optional*)
½ *cup* (112 *g.*) *chopped parsley*

Bring the chicken broth to a boil. Add the potatoes, cut leeks, carrot and macaroni. In a separate saucepan, sauté the onion and garlic in olive oil. Add to the broth and cook until tender. Before serving, crush the carrot with a fork before returning it to the soup. Add the beans. Serve with parmesan cheese.

Fish Soups

When I was a child, fish was something one had to eat on Friday nights, Christmas Eve and during Lent. Naturally, I grew up disliking fish with the exception of calamari cooked with tomatoes. As the most noble herb, sweet basil, has an affinity to the tomato, the tomato has an affinity to fish.

My introduction to the splendor of Zuppa di Pesce was at the Fisherman's Wharf in San Francisco before my departure for Japan to bring musical productions to our troops there and in Korea. The restaurants that mingled exotically on the Wharf resulted in my becoming aware of a completely new food experience. Tradition has it that the marvellous fish soups or stews evolved from the Italian fishermen cooking their meals *al fresco* on the wharves while they worked. Passers-by stopped, lured and rooted as the ancient Greek sailors had been by the enchanted singing of The Sirens. The tourists were immobilized by the enticing aromas that bubbled from the fishermen's pots. Like all Italians, the fishermen shared their food happily and thus became the first of the many *al fresco* restaurants along the wharf.

In later years I strolled along the wharves of many fish markets in port cities, especially the Mediterranean. My palate rapaciously developed a taste for the myriad combinations of white fish, shell fish and the tiny shell-encrusted short fish cooked with wine, vegetables and pasta. There are as many variations of Zuppa di Pesce as there are fishing villages. This kingly dish, hearty enough to serve as a main course with a salad of fresh greens and accompanied by crusty white bread, is one of the greatest delights of the seasoned traveler.

The recipe below is the basis for many variations. It is distinctively a sea soup, but one easily duplicated in the most land-locked community. Frozen fish is available in almost all supermarkets. The use of sea salt will enhance the flavor of frozen fish; it is not as subtle in taste as fish only one hour from the sea, but with a sensitive use of herbs and sea salt, an excellent fish soup can be prepared.

Zuppa di Pesce

3 tbsp. (45 ml.) olive oil
3 garlic cloves
8 large tomatoes, skinned and grated
6 chopped sprigs parsley
3 oz. (85 g.) tomato paste
1 large onion, minced
2 carrots, chopped
basil
2 cups (450 g.) shrimps
8 squid cut into thirds
2 cups (450 g.) short macaroni
½ cup (112 g.) green peas
1 cup (237 ml.) white wine
1 cup (237 ml.) water
1 tsp. (5 g.) crushed red pepper
1 tsp. (5 g.) sea salt
1 tsp. (5 g.) black pepper
bay leaf
sprig of thyme
1½ lb. (680 g.) white fish (cod, halibut, hake) cut into 1 inch
  (2.5 cm.) pieces
2 cups (450 g.) clams or mussels

In a large pot, sauté the garlic and onion in the olive oil.
Add the tomatoes; dilute the tomato paste with 3 oz. (90
ml.) of water and add with the herbs. Stir gently, breaking
the tomatoes into small pieces. Add the carrots, wine and
water. When the mixture begins to bubble add the white
fish. Cook the macaroni in salted boiling water until *al dente*.
Add the macaroni to the cooked white fish and add the
remaining fish and cook for 5 minutes or until the shells
steam open. If you are using canned or frozen fish add the
fish at the last minute. The peas are the last ingredient to
mix into the soup. Serve with crusty white bread. This is a
thick, rich soup and only needs a salad for a complete meal.
If you feel particularly luxurious, add crab or lobster meat
to the soup.

Calamari Soup

1 onion
2 lb. (900 g.) squid (small)
1 cup (237 ml.) white wine
1 cup (237 ml.) chicken broth
½ cup (227 g.) short-cut macaroni
6 tomatoes, peeled and quartered
1 sprig parsley
1 tbsp. (15 ml.) lemon juice
2 cloves garlic

Clean and cut the squid into 1 inch (2.5 cm.) rounds. Gently
sauté the onions, garlic and tomatoes in the olive oil. Add
the white wine, chicken broth and macaroni. Simmer for 20
minutes then add the calamari (squid) and cook for 5
minutes more. Do not overcook the little calamari or it
will take on the qualities of mature rubber! Add the lemon
juice and serve with chopped parsley.

SALADS

Some salads can be a beginning to the meal, served as a first course, a main course, or served after the main course with cheese to cleanse the palate for the coming sweet. I am most interested in the main dish or luncheon salad because our family customarily alternate between salads and soups for our midday or evening meal, depending upon the weather and contents of the refrigerator.

Americans have always been known for the ingenuity and imagination they use in creating a salad. Fresh fruits, greens, vegetables, fish, and meat combined with pasta and artistically blended can make a dish as delightful to the eye as it is to the palate. I am constantly surprised that warm weather countries do not create more interesting salads from the bounty of fresh fruits, vegetables and fish around them. The typical Mediterranean salad, Ensalada Mista—a mixture of greens, tomatoes, onions and olives, is excellent and quite refreshing as a prelude or ending to a meal. Imaginative bowls of cold fish and olives usually are available with drinks at cafés, but the salad as a one-dish meal is not commonly used.

'American Salad Bars' have been popping up on the Continent and in England, usually in department store restaurants that cater to that doyenne of shoppers—the dieting female! These tidy counters supposedly emulate the best of American food along with the hamburger heavens, southern-fried chicken emporia and ice-cream parlors that dot the business districts of many international cities. The 'American' salad consists usually of a limp piece of lettuce, a dried-out slice of ham and one of those tasteless miniscule cotton wool flavored tomatoes, especially grown to confuse the taste buds of the consumer. The salad is then arrogantly crowned with a mixture that is euphemistically called 'salad cream'. This concoction, my dears, is the nadir of salad creation. The essence of American salad-making lies in the freshness, the variety, and the combinations of ingredients.

I remember giving an 'American-styled' barbecue for my neighbors several summers ago at our home in Spain—a bit like taking snow to an Eskimo since the Spanish are the creators of the *barbecola*. The Spaniard usually builds a fire with grape vines in a discarded wheelbarrow or other metal receptacle and places the various kinds of meat, coated with olive oil, on a grill over the fire. They then toss an eggplant (aubergine) or two and sweet peppers also olive-oil coated, into the glowing coals to slowly roast as the meat is cooking.

We had brought with us a cast-iron barbecue with air vents and all the glories of American technical expertise. My guests were sufficiently impressed with this wonder and of course were too polite to say that the meats and chicken tasted much the same as their unsophisticated efforts. My only salvation as a hostess was when they brought their plates to the buffet table and saw the large variety of salads that were to accompany the barbecued meat. Our friends were delighted and intrigued with the combinations of vegetables and pasta-based salads. What intrigued them

most was the careful choice of garnishes arranged on the salads.

A salad is more attractive to the stomach if it is artistically presented. Unusually-shaped dishes enhance the appearance of a salad. The Japanese, in arranging their food on exquisitely shaped dishes, present patterns and designs evolved from the contours of the food. Selectivity in garnishes accompanying the salad are part of the art of salad making. The garnish should be fresh, of good quality and if possible cut into interesting shapes. Here are several suggestions:

— Always blanch and skin tomatoes. Tomatoes cut into wedges, diced or sliced paper-thin in rounds, are excellent garnishes.

— Radishes cut into the familiar roses and chilled are delightful. If you have a particularly elongated radish slice halfway through the thickness of the radish in an even pattern, creating a different radish garnish.

— Cut carrots into slender sticks or cut thin lengths and chill into carrot curls. Grated carrot is a very effective topping.

— Onion rings, thinly cut and separated, marinated in white wine and sugar are highly effective on a heartier salad. Pepper rings can also be prepared in this manner.

— Quartered hard-boiled eggs, devilled eggs and minced eggs add color to a salad.

— Olives, artichoke hearts, anchovy fillets and ground nuts add interest as well as a decorative garnish.

Use your imagination and color sense to make the salad an interesting as well as a delicious dish.

Following are some of the recipes I used for the Spanish party and others that my family and friends have enjoyed.

Macaroni Salad

4 *cups (900 g.) cooked short-cut macaroni*
juice of one lemon
2 *stalks celery (fresh fennel is a delightful change)*
1 *large onion, minced*
6 *scallions*
8 *eggs, devilled*
½ *green pepper, minced*
lettuce leaves
1 *cup (225 g.) mayonnaise*
2 *tsp. (10 g.) mustard*
¼ *cup (55 g.) pitted black olives*
3 *sprigs of parsley*
4 *tomatoes, skinned and cut into wedges*
1 *carrot, cut into slices*
¼ *cucumber, sliced*

Combine the mayonnaise, lemon juice and mustard in a large bowl. Lightly toss the macaroni until it is well-coated. Add the chopped raw vegetables. Arrange lettuce leaves or endive leaves on a large platter. Spoon the macaroni onto the leaves so that it forms a large sphere shaped mound. Alternate the tomato wedges and devilled eggs around the salad. Sprinkle fresh parsley over the top of the salad.

Devilled Eggs:

Slice hard-boiled eggs lengthwise. Scoop the yolk gently into a small bowl. Set the halves onto a platter. Crush the eggs with a fork, add ½ cup (112 g.) mayonnaise, 2 tsp. (10 g.) prepared mustard and blend into the crushed yolk. Fork the mixture into the halves and press your fork lengthwise across the top for an interesting pattern. Sprinkle with paprika or cut parsley for a more interesting color.

Avocado and Chicken Salad

2 *avocado pears*
2 *cups (450 g.) cooked chicken cubed*
¼ *cup (55 g.) sliced mushrooms*
water cress
½ *cup (112 g.) chopped onion*
1 *tsp. (5 g.) curry powder*
1 *cup (112 g.) mayonnaise*
1 *cup (112 g.) cooked macaroni*

Skin and cut the avocados in half. Remove the stone and peel the skin from the flesh of the avocado. Place on a bed of water cress. Mix the other ingredients and scoop into the avocado half. Garnish with more water cress. Another pungent salad green such as endive can be used.

Salads

A choice of macaroni salads—perfect for that summer luncheon or barbecue.

1. Macaroni Stuffed Tomatoes
2. Stuffed Peppers
3. Macaroni and Chicken Stuffed Avocado
4. Bean and Macaroni Salad
5. Spaghetti and Salami Salad
6. Macaroni Salad

Stuffed Peppers and Macaroni Salad

This recipe is an elegant luncheon platter that is quite substantial.

4 *large peppers*
3 *cups* (675 *g.*) *cooked macaroni*
1 (8 *oz. or* 225 *g.*) *can tuna fish*
1 *cup* (225 *g.*) *mayonnaise*
salt and pepper
1 *tsp.* (5 *g.*) *oregano*
½ *cup* (112 *g.*) *black olives*
2 *tomatoes, sliced*
4 *anchovies*

Blanch the peppers and cut lengthwise. Arrange on a bed of sliced tomatoes. Mix the macaroni, tuna fish, olives, oregano and seasonings in a small bowl. Scoop the mixture into the peppers and garnish with an anchovy fillet.

Salami and Macaroni Salad

3 *cups* (675 *g.*) *cooked macaroni*
8 *slices Italian salami*
6 *scallions*
escarole leaves
fresh parsley
½ *green pepper*
½ *cup* (118 *ml.*) *Italian salad dressing*
garlic salt and pepper
tomato wedges

Cut the Italian salami into small lengths. Chop the scallions into small pieces but do not waste the green stalks. The whole of the scallion is edible and adds a colorful tang to any salad. Blanch the pepper in boiling water, skin and then cut into small pieces. Combine all the indredients with the dressing until well-coated. Add salt and pepper to taste. Arrange on a combination of endive and escarole. Garnish with tomato wedges and artichokes. Sprinkle parsley or water cress over the top.

Shrimp and Macaroni Salad

Along the Mediterranean coast, restaurant chefs rarely shell their shrimp before presenting the dish. All recipes from fish soups to main courses arrive with the shrimp intact—containing the delicious juices within its crustacean body. Peeling the shrimp tends to be somewhat messy but the fish are far more delicate in flavor. As you gain courage you will even suck the juices from the shell with an appreciation akin to that of the most adroit gourmet.

A well-traveled English friend, the Baron Avro Manhattan, the political writer, who prides himself on his worldliness was invited to share a meal with his Spanish friends. The second course consisted of a large platter piled high with cooked, unshelled shrimp. Their tiny red feelers mingled with the dressing of crushed garlic, olive oil and parsley—a delightful sight and his gastric juices began to churn with anticipation. Our cosmopolitan friend gingerly placed several shrimp on his plate. He looked around and then solved the problem by popping the whole shrimp into his mouth and crushed away with what he considered elan. The poor dear choked! A Spanish friend, noting his discomfort politely asked if this was the way Englishmen normally ate shrimp? Our friend then observed that his dinner companions were skilfully, with a knife and fork, dismantling the shrimp into an edible form.

In the following recipe I compromise. Use cooked shelled shrimp for the main mixture and garnish with unshelled cooked shrimp for added flavor.

2 *cups* (450 *g.*) *cooked shelled shrimp*
1 *cup* (225 *g.*) *cooked unshelled shrimp*
2 *cups* (450 *g.*) *cooked shell macaroni*
1 *onion, diced*
fresh parsley
juice of one lemon
4 *tomatoes, skinned*
1 *tsp.* (5 *g.*) *crushed red pepper*
1 *cup* (237 *ml.*) *mayonnaise*
¼ *cup* (58 *ml.*) *ketchup*
salt to taste

Combine the mayonnaise, ketchup, seasonings and lemon juice in a small bowl. Set aside. Combine the shrimp, parsley and onion in a large bowl. Toss the dressing lightly until all the ingredients are well-covered. Adjust for salt. This salad is more attractive to the eye if placed in a pretty pottery bowl that will complement the color of the shrimp and dressing. After arranging the salad in a bowl, garnish with tomato and egg wedges along the edge of the dish. Arrange the unshelled shrimp in a pattern, radiating from the center of the dish.

Bean and Macaroni Salad

2 *cups* (450 *g.*) *cooked shell macaroni*
2 *cups* (450 *g.*) *cooked beans* (*white kidney or ceci*)
2 *onions, chopped*
½ *cup* (118 *ml.*) *olive oil*
¼ *cup* (58 *ml.*) *vinegar*
½ *tsp.* (2.5 *g.*) *oregano*
1 *tbsp.* (14 *g.*) *parsley*
1 *tsp.* (5 *g.*) *sweet basil*
½ *tsp.* (2.5 *g.*) *crushed red pepper*
salt

Combine the beans, macaroni and onions in a bowl. Mix the olive oil, vinegar and herbs in another bowl and whisk. Add to the ingredients, chill, and serve on a strongly-flavored salad green (escarole, endive, Chinese cabbage or water cress).

Macaroni Salad with Tuna Fish and Anchovies

3 *cups* (675 *g.*) *cooked short-cut macaroni*
2 (6 *oz.* or 170 *g.*) *cans tuna fish*
½ *cup* (118 *ml.*) *olive oil*
2 *tbsp.* (30 *ml.*) *wine vinegar*
1 *cup* (225 *g.*) *parsley, chopped*
3 *garlic cloves, minced*
½ *cup* (118 *ml.*) *mayonnaise*
10 *anchovy fillets*

In a bowl, mix the tuna fish and oil with the olive oil. Mash the tuna into a fine paste (the blender is a help here). Slowly add the vinegar, garlic cloves and mayonnaise. Stir until well-blended. Mix the macaroni and tuna mixture. Place on a platter and garnish with anchovy fillets and parsley. Chill for 4 hours before serving.

Stuffed Tomatoes

The height of the summer growing season presents us with the succulent beef-steak tomato—rich in color and juices, with a genuine tomato taste and not the cardboard version served in the depths of winter. A large tomato, well-stuffed, accompanied by bread and wine is a delightful summer lunch.

The following includes a variety of stuffings to fill four large beef-steak tomatoes.

Stuffing Number 1 — Macaroni Salad

4 *large beef-steak tomatoes*
4 *cups (900 g.) macaroni salad*

Scald the tomatoes and peel. Place on lettuce leaves, endive, escarole, or water cress (combinations of these can be arranged on the platter for a more delightful taste.) Cut the top from the tomato and scoop the hard center core from the fruit. Place 1 cup (225 g.) macaroni salad in each tomato and cover with the top of the tomato.

Stuffing Number 2 — Lentils, Fennel and Ketchup

1 *cup (225 g.) cooked lentils*
2 *cups (450 g.) macaroni*
1 *onion, sliced*
1 *tsp. (5 g.) oregano*
½ *fresh fennel cut into small pieces*
salt and pepper
½ *cup (118 ml.) olive oil*
2 *tbsp. (30 ml.) ketchup*
crushed clove of garlic

In making this dressing I usually utilize the last dredge in a ketchup bottle. If there is approximately 2 tbsp. (30 ml.) in the bottle I add ½ cup (118 ml.) oil and ¼ cup (60 ml.) of vinegar, salt, pepper, crushed garlic and shake vigorously until blended.

Combine the cooked lentils, macaroni, onion, oregano and fennel. Mix ½ cup (120 ml.) of the prepared dressing with the macaroni mixture. Scoop into the prepared tomatoes and serve.

Stuffing Number 3 — Tuna and Anchovies

2 *cups (450 g.) cooked short-cut macaroni*
1 *(8 oz. or 225 g.) can tuna fish*
1 *can anchovies*
green olives
1 *onion, sliced*
2 *tbsp. (30 ml.) olive oil*
1 *tbsp. (15 ml.) vinegar*
salt and pepper
3 *tsp. (15 g.) fresh cut parsley*

Mix the macaroni shells with the tuna fish, cut onion, salt, pepper, olive oil, vinegar and parsley. Spoon into the prepared tomatoes. Place on a platter and garnish with an anchovy fillet curled around a pitted green olive.

Cold White Fish and Macaroni Salad

2 *cups (450 g.) spaghetti, cooked*
3 *tomatoes, skinned and sliced*
1 *cup (225 g.) black olives*
2 *onions, sliced*
2 *cloves garlic*
½ *cup (120 ml.) white wine or dry vermouth*
salt
1 *lb. (454 g.) white fish (cod, haddock, halibut)*
fresh parsley
fresh basil
¼ *cup (58 ml.) olive oil*
2 *tbsp. (30 ml.) vinegar*
1 *tbsp. (15 ml.) ketchup*
½ *tsp. (2.5 g.) crushed red pepper*

Poach the fish in white wine or vermouth. Break the fish into chunk-size pieces. Arrange the spaghetti on a platter. Do not handle the fish too much as you put it on the spaghetti (it should be in bite-sized pieces). Arrange the tomato slices, onions and black olives over the top of the fish. Cut sweet basil and parsley into a garnish for the top of the salad. Mix the olive oil, vinegar and ketchup, crushed garlic, salt and crushed red pepper in a bowl. Pour over the salad. With a fork, gently move the spaghetti to ensure that the dressing covers the mixture. Chill for 2 hours and serve.

Stuffed Calamari Salad

8 *large calamari (squid)*
1 *cup (225 g.) cooked pastina*
½ *cup (120 ml.) white wine*
1 *cup (237 ml.) chicken bouillon*
¼ *cup (58 ml.) olive oil*
1 *tbsp. (15 ml.) lemon juice*
1 *tbsp. (14 g.) salt*
2 *tbsp. (28 g.) capers*
1 *chopped, skinned tomato*
2 *spring onions, chopped*
1 *clove garlic*
½ *tsp. (2.5 g.) nutmeg*
1 *cup (225 g.) chopped cooked spinach*
2 *tbsp. (30 ml.) olive oil*
½ *tbsp. (7.5 ml.) vinegar*

Clean the calamari. Try not to break the body; remove the head from the tentacles and skin the fish. Place in a shallow pan with the wine and bouillon. Add a clove of garlic and bring to a boil and simmer gently for just 10 minutes, until done. Drain and place on a platter. In a small bowl combine the pastina, tomato, onion, spinach and marjoram. Pour ¼ cup (58 ml.) olive oil over the mixture. Stir until blended. Combine the vinegar, 1 tbsp. (15 ml.) olive oil and capers. Arrange the calamari on a platter. Cover with the olive oil sauce. Marinade in the refrigerator for an hour. Serve with onion slices.

Macaroni Stuffed Eggplant Salad

1 *large eggplant (aubergine)*
1 *cup (225 g.) cooked ditali*
½ *cup (112 g.) sliced mushrooms*
1 *large onion, chopped*
3 *cloves garlic*
1 *tsp. (5 g.) marjoram*
2 *tbsp. (30 ml.) olive oil*
¼ *cup (58 ml.) olive oil*
1 *lemon*
parsley
salt and pepper
½ *tsp. (5 g.) sugar*

Boil the eggplant for 20 minutes. It is easier if you cut a slab from the side. When it is cool remove the pulp from the eggplant but be sure to leave a firm shell to stuff. In a small frying pan gently sauté the onion and garlic. Mix and add the cooked macaroni. Slowly pour the olive oil, stirring at the same time, into the mixture. Add the juice of a lemon. Stir and stuff the eggplant shell. Garnish with parsley and chill for one hour before serving.

REMEMBERED FEASTS

We love to entertain! Invitations for Sunday lunch, an evening's meal or a holiday feast—breaking bread with friends—is definitely fun time. Although I plan *all* our meals in advance, preparations for dinner parties and buffets start with the first invitation. Lists of supplies based on the menu are written in great detail; a cooking schedule is worked out so that the food can be prepared over a three-to-four day period before the party. All food, with the exception of adding the dressing to the salad, is done before the first guests arrive. The table is set, the bar prepared, the food ready to be served at least an hour before time. In fact, we usually have a quick lie-down before dressing for the party. I loathe attending parties when the host or hostess appears exhausted, still adjusting his or her party clothes with that harassed expression of 'I'll never do it again!' as they answer the doorbell to greet guests.

Of course, pasta casseroles are ideal for entertaining. Usually, pasta appears either as a second course or the entree. Holiday meals are the easiest to plan because so many traditional foods are involved. Our friends begin ringing a month in advance to ensure that the festivity is to take place as usual! We have a core of close friends who form the nucleus of every party. We all like to eat and talk; we all share the same love of 'show biz' music from the forties and fifties that results in virtuoso performances around the piano that I am sure sends all the local cats scurrying for shelter! The complete guest list grows from this jolly group to include visiting friends or relatives, recent contacts in our professional lives and neighbors (it is safer to have them join in rather than shout, later).

We usually plan three or four major parties a year. Most of our married life has been spent abroad and sentimentality and nostalgia for family oriented parties run rampant at holidays. We are authorities on surrogate family holidays. Americans are always on the move—many of you are probably dispersed about the countryside and worlds away from the roots of the familial holiday table. We Americans are known for our hospitality and generosity so it is very easy to become, as part of this tradition, the *Perle Mesta* of your community.

Somehow, regardless of the city or country where we have lived, our parties usually include spontaneous entertainment. For example, the odd fire or two, halfway through the meal, brings out the best, not only in your guests but in the Fire Departments of the world. We had, many years ago, a tiny flat in a recently converted Greenwich Village walk-up. At one Christmas Eve party our prized 'convenience' (the miniscule fireplace) burst forth into an unexpected glow. Smoke poured down the chimney defying all previously held concepts of gravity. The Fire Department was called. They mingled with raised hatchets amongst the guests and chopped away at the now enflamed wall. A visit to our upstairs neighbor proved to be the source of the fire. Indulging in the Christmas spirit, the young bachelor was vainly burning a huge yule log over a bed of several rolled up *New York Times*' Sunday editions. It was beyond the fireplace's ability to co-operate. For some architecturally unknown reason the smoke and sparks descended, adding to the heat of our festivities. For months afterwards the plastered-in hole was humanized with a caricature of our mutual landlord by an artist friend commemorating the event and the landlord's lack of haste in repainting the wall.

Several years ago we had invited twenty-five assorted souls to our annual Thanksgiving bash in our London apartment. The living room had been cleared of the larger pieces of furniture and a rented table was covered with the best of our linens, crystal, china and silver. It was, generally speaking, an 'all stops out' party. The two musicians whom we generally have at our larger efforts were tuning their instruments—for some unknown reason they had come dressed as gypsies. My daughter had been finalizing a flower arrangement on the table when she announced to her father, quietly, as he served cocktails to our guests in the library, that the draperies in the living room were on fire! All doors were immediately closed. The guests, thinking it a prank, converged onto the fire stairs in the hallway. The firemen arrived—ten, strong, 6-foot giants along with several policemen and a beautifully groomed policewoman.

My husband's agent, arriving a bit late, rang the bell of our apartment and when a smoke-smeared, mascara-dripping policewoman opened the door he said brightly 'Oh, are we doing it in drag, dear?' The slammed door only confused him further until he sighted the now-aware but laughing crowd at the end of the corridor. Once the fire was under control we trooped back into the flat to continue our party of Thanksgiving.

The living room was a burnt-out shell. The dreary, misty English November afternoon—now very much in evidence without a cheerful covering of draperies—glared through the blown out windows.

The ventian blinds, minus their silk cords, lay heaped on the floor. Watered smoke-smears dripped from the walls. Lamps, shaded only by wire circles darkened the room with a meager light from soot-encrusted bulbs. Our newly hung Joe Tilson painting, purchased the day before, drooped on the wall with its pop art plastic frame melted. Our rugs had been thrown out the windows and the firemen were cleaning the water soaked parquet floor. To my everlasting admiration, the English firemen had not broken one plate, glass or serving dish on the table. Our total loss, other than cleaning and redecorating the room, was a wooden pepper mill! The guests stripped the table, washed the dishes and sat down to devour the Thanksgiving feast to the accompaniment of the wild violin music from the relieved musicians. The English artist, Lucien Frend, arrived halfway through the meal and murmured as he entered the room 'What a charming flat. Unusual decor'.

Our darling, wire-haired Daschund, Tiger Italiano Butterscotch Galloper (the outburst of an eight-year-old's joy with her first dog) had wagged his friendly tail too vigorously and knocked over a fragile lamp that I had placed on the floor, behind the draperies—for safety!

My love of parties, of course, is based on the many gatherings I remember as a child. My parents entertained frequently. We gathered at relative's homes for some of our traditional holiday meals. Friends and their families joined us for wonderful picnics in the lake district of the Adirondack Mountains. Every conceivable occasion was celebrated; parties were planned not only for adventures in eating but for entertainment as well .Home-brewed musicians, singing, parlor games and card playing were mustered for at-home events and races, food, boating and swimming dominated the outdoor activities. In the winter months several families hired a sled on Sunday evenings. Well-insulated in snow-suits and blankets we tucked ourselves into the warmth of the hay. The driver smartly drove the sleigh across the frost-encrusted snow; we sang all the old familiar songs—our voices rang out in discordant harmony shattering the crystal cold night air. Usually we ended the evening at our home, appetites fully honed, for one of my mother's marvellous spaghetti suppers.

An Italian-American Christmas Eve

I remember with nostalgia, Christmas Eve with Aunt Theresa. From the below-zero temperature of an upstate New York December, we entered her home through the back door into a warm, deliciously scented kitchen. Exuberant shouts of many children greeted a cousin, announced the latest arrival. Strident, excited women's voices issued commands. The men's voices were already softened by their indulgence of Christmas cheer. We paraded snow through the dining room, hurriedly 'unlayering' the coats, sweaters, scarves, ski-pants and stadium boots on our way to the bedroom and heaped the discarded garments onto the mountain of apparel on the bed. We quickly glimpsed the tree in the parlor twinkling a welcome in the darkened room. Presents, forbidden until midnight, lay seductively under the tree.

We were then sorted out according to age and table. As you progressed in years you graduated from the kitchen table—oh, blessed day—to the main table in the dining room. Aunts, uncles, cousins sat about the table, talking, singing and teasing each other with the abandonment that only close families endure. The table was dominated by large bowls of spaghetti, covered with a succulent Baccala sauce. Plates of pepper-seasoned orange slices dressed with garlic and olive oil, black-roasted eels brought up hot from the coal furnace snugly curled in small dishes, golden fried fish balls, stuffed calamari, salads, fresh Italian bread, tangerines and grapes and jugs of red wine surrounded the spaghetti. One's eye jumped to the sideboard where crisply fried lover's knots covered with honey and powdered sugar, rings of tiny pastry balls encrusted with multicolored candies and almonds and those wonderful raisin and cinnamon cakes awaited their turn and teased the appetite.

Wine-laughter grew louder with the evening's progression towards midnight. We dashed into the bitter cold to attend the midnight church service. On our return, cups of thick, black coffee sweetened with anisette were sipped. The delicious liquid flowed down, warming every chilled muscle and cold bone. The chaos of Christmas wrappings, hurriedly torn inevitably revealed another scarf or pair of woollen mittens. Soon it was time to end the party. The younger children who had earlier burrowed into the layers of coats piled on the bed were gently awakened, scooped from their lairs, only to doze against their parents' bodies as limp arms and legs were slipped into warm coats and leggings.

Cheerful bursts of Christmas carols followed us from the warmth of the family gathering, cocooning our family until we reached the security of our own beds and dreams of Christmas morning. Our Christmas Eves have followed the same pattern: a mixture of delicious food, friends, music and the joyful cold walk to church for the celebration of Christmas. Somehow it has never completely emulated the original—perhaps I have not relaxed my guests sufficiently to dunk orange segments into their wine with sufficient gusto!

An 80th Birthday Celebration

Several years ago when my father was approaching his eightieth birthday, letters were arriving in London reporting the plans for the coming event. We felt we really could not travel halfway around the world to attend the coming birthday celebration in good conscience, for the week available to us between university terms and acting engagements. We prepared to enjoy the event, secondhand, through letters, feeling very sorry for ourselves indeed.

However, two weeks before the day, a letter arrived from my mother, giving details of the luncheon she was planning for the twenty guests: a buffet of ham, turkey, salads, barbecued chicken and the birthday cake. As I read the letter the adrenaline raced to my heart and then sank into the depths of my stomach. Buffet? Baked ham and turkey for my 'Wop Pop'? Potato salad for my 'Dago Dad'? I knew and appreciated the rationale behind the menu—my mother is only two years behind my father in reaching eighty and of course she chose a menu that would be easy to prepare and serve. I overreacted with all the zeal of the Lone Ranger riding to the rescue. My father's greatest joy is to sit for hours at the table surrounded by Italian food, wine and his family. 'I must go to Texas and cook the birthday dinner! Daddy must have an Italian feast!' My husband and daughter immediately agreed to join me on the trip. They never miss a party!

It was a grand occasion.

My daughter and I lovingly cooked for three days preparing the meal. The final morning found all the women, sisters, cousins, daughters and mothers shouting directions to each other at cross purposes as we finalized the preparations. My daughter who has not had my conditioning in an Italian-American household was at first cowed by the frenetic Italian cheerfulness. Finally she perched herself on a ladder, tying balloons and flowers to the chandelier and outshouted her female relatives with instinctive zest. Blood will tell!

We sat down to a seven-course meal—banquet! My cousin had brought fresh fish from the Gulf coast and we started with seafood poached in piquant tomato sauce. My daughter and I had rolled out 125 cannelloni, stuffed the squares with venison, covered with bechamel sauce and served them, bubbling with butter and parmesan cheese as the second course. We followed with spaghetti, steak pizzaoli, chicken and peppers and fillet of pork with artichokes. Salads, cheeses and fresh fruit followed to cleanse our palates for the wonderfully rich, rum-soaked birthday cake and champagne. We sat at the table seven indulgent hours, eating, drinking, reminiscing—truly celebrating my father's eighty years in a manner that he had raised us to enjoy. It was indeed a memorable feast.

Party Picnics

The contents of picnic baskets can arouse great passions. Some schools of thought support the tuna-fish-salad-sandwich school, some the exquisitely-canned-gourmet-food school; and some the warm-casserole-salad-and-fresh-bread school of thought. I belong firmly in the latter tradition. The picnics of my youth, centered around large baking dishes filled with stuffed macaroni, fried chicken and peppers, macaroni salads, fresh Italian bread, fruit of the season and cheese. For a short period in my life I lapsed into the sandwich school from sheer laziness. An incident in Spain, where picnicking has become a fine art, aroused my dormant instincts.

We were visiting Monserrat, the inspiring serrated mountain that thrusts upwards from the plains of Catalonia, dominating the horizon from Barcelona to Tarragona. The cable-car had lurched us upwards to an ideal picnic area above the Monastery. As I unwrapped our hurriedly prepared lunch of sodden tuna fish sandwiches I noticed my family looking longingly at the table next to ours. A Spanish family was busily devouring macaroni with a meat sauce, chicken, salads and freshly cut bread as they appeared on the table from the various containers in the picnic hamper. I certainly did not receive a star on my chart for family management that day! Gloomily, my family tucked into the worn-out sandwiches, casting sulky looks my way. The grass was definitely greener on the opposite side of the fence. Never again! We troop forth with well chosen provisions now.

Many of the recipes I have included in this book are eminently suitable for picnics. They travel well, retain their freshness and are delicious eaten luke-warm or cold. Obviously the salads are quite portable. I carry soups in a wide-mouthed Thermos for easy pouring. Casseroles such as rigatoni and ricotta, lasagne, macaroni and eggplant and rigatoni Milanese are excellent. One of our favorite warm weather picnic dishes is summer spaghetti—lightly laced with tuna fish, fresh tomatoes, olive oil and black olives. A spaghetti omelette is another appetizing dish, especially if you add mushrooms or left-over meatballs.

For some picnics, I arrange the food on the plates before departure, covering them with aluminium foil. I must say though, there is no substitute for the old-fashioned wicker picnic hamper. It is an investment that gives many years of ease and enjoyment in picnicking pleasure. A colorful cloth spread on a table or the ground, pretty dishes and the food packed conveniently for easy service are the basis of a good picnic. Many families carry collapsible chairs and a small, collapsible table in the trunks of their cars so that the picnic spot can be spontaneously chosen for the panoramic view rather than the need for an organized picnic area.

Picnic foods should be varied, easily served, well seasoned and attractive to the eye. My ecology-minded daughter always remembers a trash bag for the inevitable scraps, leaving the picnic area as lovely as we found it. Try wandering from your backyard barbecue into the countryside and rediscover memories of your youth. It is a moveable feast.

Leona's Party Lasagne—A Memorable Feast (*overleaf*)
Pepertoni, Lasagne and Macaroni Loaf make an excellent choice for a festive occasion.

INDEX

Note—The mention of a specific type of pasta in a recipe title does *not* mean that it is the *only* one which can be used. Any related type or size of pasta can be substituted if desired.